Gracias

Other works by Alma Luz Villanueva:

Short Fiction

Weeping Woman: La Llorona and Other Stories

Novels

The Ultraviolet Sky
Naked Ladies
Luna's California Poppies
Song of the Golden Scorpion

Poetry

Mother, May I?
Life Span
Blood Root
Planet
Vida
Desire
Soft Chaos

Gracias

new poems

Alma Luz Villanueva

WingsPress

San Antonio, TX

2015

Gracias © 2015 by Alma Luz Villanueva

Cover photograph by the author.

First Edition

Print Edition ISBN: 978-1-60940-395-9
ePub ISBN: 978-1-60940-396-6
MobiPocket / Kindle ISBN: 978-1-60940-397-3
PDF ISBN: 978-1-60940-398-0

Wings Press
627 E. Guenther
San Antonio, Texas 78210
Phone/fax: (210) 271-7805

On-line catalogue and ordering:
www.wingspress.com
All Wings Press titles are distributed to the trade by
Independent Publishers Group
www.ipgbook.com

Library of Congress Cataloging-in-Publication Data:

Villanueva, Alma, 1944-
[Poems. Selections]
Gracias : new poems / Alma Luz Villanueva. -- First edition.
    pages ; cm
    ISBN 978-1-60940-395-9 (softcover) -- ISBN 978-1-60940-396-6
(epub ebook) -- ISBN 978-1-60940-397-3 (kindle-mobipocket ebook)
-- ISBN 978-1-60940-398-0 (library pdf ebook)
    I. Title.
    PS3572.I354A6 2015
    811'.54--dc23
                              2014034444

CONTENTS

I. COZCACUAUTZ

II. BUDDHA

III. FLOWER

IV. FRAGILE SILK

DEDICATORIAS

GRACIAS a mi Mamacita, Jesus Villanueva, full blood Yaqui, curandera de Sonora, México; she gave me poetry.

GRACIAS to my grandfather, Pablo Villanueva, who wrote and published poetry, owned his own newspaper, earned a Ph.D., Baptist minister.

GRACIAS mi madre, Lydia Villanueva, who carried me out of Louisiana, my racist father's family, as a toddler, 1946, to the arms of mi Mamacita, my teacher. And who woke me as girl, the early years, playing Chopin on her rented piano.

GRACIAS a mi tia, Ruth Villanueva, who told me all the family stories with laughter and tears. Feeding me fresh tortillas, delicious food, whenever I arrived.

GRACIAS a mi tio, Ruben Villanueva, gifted violinist who played entire concerts by heart — mi Mamacita's treasured son who left the body at twenty-one. Who sings through my blood and my words, Ruben.

GRACIAS a mi padre (step/real padre), Lewis 'Whitey' McSpadden, from New México, that earth — who respected my 12-year-old warrior spirit that first meeting and nurtured that spirit, my childhood into womanhood, all of his life.

GRACIAS a la madre de mi Mamacita, Ysidra, full blood Yaqui, well known curandera de Sonora, who named her daughter Jesus, not the feminine Jesusa — who married five times, "Each time a better man." Mi tia Ruth told me the story, quoting her, making me laugh. Her strength is in my pen, gracias.

As Mamacita would declare in moments of sorrow/joy — "The Yaquis are undefeated!" (in Spanish) Her eagle eyes revealed, on fire. Her loud gritos when we danced to rancheras on the radio, laughing. The 'old Yaqui woman' who was seen in public was not the warrior/dreamer I knew in private, just us.

GRACIAS to all the ancestors, dead or alive, the next seven generations.

GRACIAS to all of my four beloved, now grown, children, who taught me to love, in a blind extension of love.

And GRACIAS to Bryce Milligan por todo.

Alma Luz Villanueva
San Miguel de Allende
México
The Sixth Sacred Sun

I.

Cozcacuautz

COZCACUAUTZ

(Gran Señora Aguila de Coatl —
Great Woman of Eagle/Snake)

I follow a Mayan man in
traditional dress to a place with
a beautiful fountain — he
draws me in, tells me my
name by the sacred Mayan
Calendar — Cozcacuautz, that
I'm a great philosopher, that
I don't speak with my mouth but
with words on a page, but I
do sing, he laughs, that I
can't bear my freedom to be
taken, that I must travel, that
I must not live in the past, "Vive
en el momento, que hermosa estas,"
I laugh. He gives me a pouch with
eagle/snake, stones for my journey, my
name, as he blows on a conch
shell, gazing into my eyes, I
gaze back, we create this
moment, quickly he kisses
me on the lips, blowing
his breath into me, smiling
like Quetzalcoatl, his eyes
twin suns. "Gracias," I whisper.

Waking dream ... he tells me so much more.

San Miguel de Allende, México
2006

LA POCHA LOCA

I go to watch
tango in my warm
UGG boots, winter
in San Miguel, to

find they're teaching
tango, a handsome
young man my youngest
son's age — the waitress

talks me into it, I
sit and wait my
turn, it's the
connection, "Es

la conexion, asi," he
places my hands on
his chest, tells me
to push, used to

play with my sons,
I almost push him
over, we laugh,
we dance the tango,

very basic, first
time for me, then
a bit more complex,
my open hands

pushing on his chest —
I make a circle with
my arms, he ducks
under, "La conexion,"

he laughs, I'm
getting better in my
clunky, warm boots,
he speaks to me in

Spanish, my body
remembers my childhood
words, next my tongue,
he tells me to drink

lots of tequila, it'll
flow, we laugh as
he leads me backwards,
a la tango, people

are staring, la conexion,
joy and play, the one
I've had with my
sons — someone else's

turn, he tells me I'm
a good dancer, "No,
no," I laugh, "Si, si,"

he smiles, ten minutes
later he returns to
dance with La Pocha
Loca in her clunky

UGG boots, the other
dancers in spiky,
sexy heels, I make
a circle with my

hands, he ducks under,
we laugh, I cross
my left foot over,
shift my weight, dance

backwards a la tango —
Pochita Loca, my bullfighting

cousin, Chula, used to tease me,
she visiting from México, pocha

(discolored, faded), a Mexican born
in the USA. Now, I understand
how I need the rainbow, to dance
backwards a la tango, open hands,

la conexion, I'm thirsty. For color.

*Finnegan's Bar with a nod to James Joyce, and
and the bartender, Patrick, who spoke
perfect Spanish with an Irish accent.*

San Miguel de Allende, México
December 2004

GRACIAS

"Alma Luz, with a name like
that, go," he laughs,
waving me through the
final border, Juarez, to the Sun,

I crossed into the rainbow —

Sold washer/dryer, gave my
favorite black leather couch
to Goodwill, the Guatemalan
has a large family, "Take it,"

I crossed into the rainbow —

The Canadian Indian says he
crossed, "As long as the water
flows, you know that unbroken treaty,"
he laughs, likes the CD player, "Take it,"

I crossed into the rainbow —

I give my treasured books to my
son, Marco, takes the tin orange
ladle I made pancakes with 35 years
ago, "An heirloom," he laughs,

I crossed into the rainbow—

In El Paso, lost, trying to
find the crossing, a one legged
man pushes his wheel chair up a
curb, no one helps him in USA,

I crossed into the rainbow —

Spit into Juarez, lost, trying to
find the rainbow crossing, I run

a stop sign, cop comes running, I run
toward him, "Where?" "There," he laughs,

I crossed into the rainbow —

Wide stretches of desert, so
dry even bugs no longer splatter
my windshield, an old man kissed
white by sand laughs into the Sun —

I crossed into the rainbow —

Small towns, celebrations of
people, water, food, children
leap in play, a man in a wheel
chair takes a toll at his tope —

I crossed into the rainbow —

Mexican men eye me, pocha,
loca, mas gringa, si
señora — some flirt, some sweet,
some hate what I've become,

I crossed into the rainbow —

Mexican women size me
up, am I someone's mother,
just another pocha, gringa, puta trying
their men on like shoes, some smile hola,

I crossed into the rainbow —

High winds, small tornadoes
whip the desert, lifting my car
slightly, I'm so alive, they
hiss, we travel side by side, so alive.

I crossed into the rainbow —

I arrived in the time of
blossoming purple trees,

from my roof top they
laugh on the hillsides,

I crossed into the rainbow —

I arrived in the time of
high April winds, the
roof door slamming shut,
brick breaking glass open,

I crossed into the rainbow —

Violet twilight: gliding, white egrets,
cranes, flocks of birds in long,
trailing formations, wing to
their nightly nests at the lake,

I crossed into the rainbow —

On the street below my roof teens, families,
women in groups, walk close to the houses,
these narrow cobblestone streets, to the plaza, fire
eaters, drummers, mimes, mariachis, food from carts,

I crossed into the rainbow —

The young crescent moon finds
her place in the sky, tomorrow
the rising, real Sun, children
will walk to the milk truck with buckets,

I crossed into the rainbow —

The crescent moon digs her prongs into
my dreaming head, somewhere
teens will light fireworks all
night and the young cop will smile,

I crossed into the rainbow—

San Miguel is deep into these wild
mountains like my old home in the

Sierras, where love always found
me, here the eyes are untamed, wild,

I crossed into the rainbow —

Here, old women in rainbow
rebozos are my grandmother,
Jesus, I buy calla lilies from some, roses
from a man who calls them his queens,

I crossed into the rainbow —

Last night, at twilight as the
church bells struck seven
times, my neighbors sang a
song of lament, joy, gratitude,

I crossed into the rainbow —

Tomorrow my neighbor's rooster,
the Mexican Sun, will snatch me
from dreams, now a soft teasing night
wind coaxes the southern stars to shimmer,

I crossed into the rainbow —

Mamacita, do you finally feel
at home, your children, your
people, your language, my first
language, your dreams so alive,

We crossed into the rainbow —

I gaze at the southern stars, below
the Tropic of Cancer, I've
never seen these constellations so
clearly, your constellations, Mamacita,

We crossed into the rainbow —

Someone drives by playing U-2,
I begin to smile, every star

belongs in the Sun/Moon Sky,
and I'm at home, so alive, in this world, now

and I've crossed, oh I've crossed, into the rainbow,

Mamacita, a pure white dove visits
at twilight, I know you're free in the
wind, kissed by the
desert, twirled by tornadoes,

I hear you singing in Yaqui, Spanish, as
church bells ring, my neighbor's song,
something so beautiful, lament
and joy at once, yes, gratitude,

the crescent moon will follow me all
night as you sing in the heart of the
pure white dove. In the morning a
man will pass my door playing music to

dance to and I will give him ten pesos,
my door flung open,
I live in the rainbow, this world, and
I know my youngest son is not dying in

the current insanity (though other sons, daughters
are), the sad color code of my country; I will see
the sacred seventh generation in my
granddaughter's child,

lament and joy, joy and lament,
I sing so softly, my doors
flung open to the murmur of
Spanish, uncensored song, laughter,

life unedited,
spectrum, this
living rainbow, this
living world, singing, *gracias.*

San Miguel de Allende, México, April 2005

QUE BONITO

I saw a woman with a rainbow of
roses on her back at the
corner of my street —
I saw a tired child today, a Mayan

boy of maybe seven, resting
with his wares in a damp
doorway, and I swear
I saw his Death kiss him

gently on his left cheek —
I was buying dried fuchsia
flowers from a woman who
looked a little like mi Tia,

and when I turned to walk
over, see if he was hungry,
he was gone (did Death kiss
his other cheek?) — my children

were never tired, maybe sick a
few days then back to their
true job of wearing me out
daily, also bringing me so much

joy I wanted to live — in the
market a small boy sold me
Chiclets, pointed to some
fruit, and as I paid for

our fruit he paid me with
the most joyous smile,
making me want to live. A
beautiful man with a corrected

harelip makes me pause to see
his paintings — wedding scene, the

village surrounding bride and
groom, dark night with full

moon, a blue lake beneath
and huge, golden fish leaping
in the night sky, glowing with
moonlight — he tells me his

name, Carmelo, that he painted
these, that they sell for more in
the stores, "Que bonito," I
say and his smile is

perfect. Death will kiss us
all on both cheeks, some
still in the womb dreaming, some
over a hundred, dreaming their lives

for the first time — when Death
comes to kiss me, I will sing
him a poem and when he
murmurs, "Que bonito," I will

laugh and smile perfectly.

San Miguel de Allende
July 2005

THE TREE IN FRONT

The children on my street, in
San Miguel de Allende, play
GOOOOAAALLL until 10 pm
or so — it irritates me some

times, that long ass shout, but
mostly I love that children can
play outside till 10 pm on my street
GOOOAAALL ...

In the plaza families gather, kids running
all over till midnight or so,
fire eaters, drummers, mimes and
mariachis roam, a few pesos

in the hat, no Swat Teams,
cops in up-tight poses, just one
young cop strolling through the
plaza smiling, people constantly

talking to him (I bet they know
his mama y papa). I walk
home at night, midnight, 1am or
so, women walking in pairs, groups, alone,

a regular event for them, I tremble with
joy, trying to relax my kung fu
gait (as I did in Bali when I
realized I was scaring people, the

gentle men who wear flowers behind their
ears). I'm still jumpy but happy, walking
to mi casita on calle Orizaba, and there's
two same addresses on my street, mine

has the tree in front where people stop to
sit under, rest, their conversation
floating into my ears, and some
times the kids' ball gets stuck in

my tree, they knock laughing, as
it falls they yell in unison
GOOOAAALLL ... I still sleep with
my Buck Knife unsheathed on my night

table (I always do when I backpack
or sleep alone). I think of
women in the large cities of my
country, women in veils, in war

zones all over my planet, and their
terrified children — a friend who
interviewed women in Rwanda after the
genocide said children were forced to

cut off their parent's hands. I enter
my Orizaba casita with the tree in
front, maybe the kids are still
playing, maybe they're finally

silent, dreaming, and I sing in one long breath
GOOOOOAAAAALLLLL

San Miguel de Allende
June 2005

CROSSING INTO THE RAINBOW

I miss the morning sounds of
roosters, dogs, children's
voices, the soft Indian
laughter so early on their

way to treasured work, the
old women wrapped in deep
purple, fuchsia, lime green rebozos,
sweeping cobblestone streets, the

young man selling buckets of
coiled, white lilies, the young
Mexican boy selling rainbows of
roses spread on just washed

cobblestone, the sound of
my neighbor's vibrating, irritating,
early morning ranchera music
until I realize I'm dancing,

I laugh, walk to the plaza,
place some pesos in the
old Indian woman's gnarled,
arthritic hands (I know to

look for her, right here), she
blesses me, an equal exchange,
I buy unneeded chiclets from small
Indian children, 5 pesos, until my

change runs out, a white woman
stops me, "These kids should
be in school, not begging,"
she hasn't seen them

run to their mothers, laughing,
placing the pesos in her handsbefore
I can say, "Will you
pay for their schooling, their

daily care, food ..." She
turns on her high heels and
leaves, I force myself not to
yell, "GO FUCK YOUR SELF,"

instead I whisper, "I hope
the cobbles get your
fancy shoes ..." then, the
sight of a gigantic horse,

shaggy, huge hooves, well
groomed, saddle on the back
waiting for riders, his caretaker
holding a large tin bucket under

his huge penis as a forceful
stream of hot piss, morning
cold, steam rising, makes a
waterfall sound, I look

away, look back, smile,
the street, these children,
the old woman, the Indian
mothers wrapped in rainbows, my

irritating, so alive neighbors, the teen
selling his hand woven rainbow bracelets,
his smile as I buy a bunch for family,
friends, myself, they all bless me, the

Spirit of the house, la casita, I dreamt
she blessed me (she, covered in
rainbows) — hold the door open,
I'm coming home.

Santa Fe, New México, to Miguel de Allende
January 2005

CANTA, NO LLORES
(Sing, Don't Weep)

The woman in rainbows (the Spirit
of this house, this place, in San Miguel)
arrives in dreams — she's middle-aged,
commanding, full of authority, and
she chides me for my mediocre Spanish,
yet she knows I understand
every thing said, my childhood
tongue — "Your language will
get worse before it gets better,"
she laughs, "then you will
write the novel of your
dreams, pocha loca mia,
and I will whisper in your
seashell ear each night in
dreams, when you wake,
welcome pochita loca,
canta, no llores, canta, no llores,
si, canta, no llores ..."
sounds of Spanish on the street, children
playing, roosters crowing, dogs barking,
rancheras, and the woman in rainbows,
dreaming me, whispering in
my seashell ear, "Canta, no
llores, canta, no llores, pochita
loca, mia, en el arco iris."*

*Dream, San Miguel de Allende
December 2004*

* "Canta, no llores," from my grandmother, Jesus, her favorite song,
Cielito Lindo — I can still hear her singing it. My son, Jules, her great-
grandson, and I sang it together Christmas Eve at el Jardin, the plaza, in
San Miguel de Allende, with the joyous crowd.

OUT OF THE WINGS

Teenagers playing with
fire, drummers singing
their hands raw, African,
Middle Eastern music, these

Mexican kids roam the
country days before Christmas
Eve — my 23 year old son and
I enter the morning plaza,

three young men dressed in
black/white, sacred clowns of
life/death, they shout, sing the
words of Pablo Neruda, one

sings, the other two die, rest,
taking turns, coming back to
life, singing Neruda's words
of sky, sea, stone, simple

love — out of the wings, an
older man, 80s, steps
forward to the edge of
the stone stairs, begins

to sing his own truth,
his own tribute to
life/death and no one
calls 911, the police do

not take him away,
no one jeers (except for
the staring tourists, embarrassed),
people pause to listen, slight shake

of head in sympathy, Yes
that's how la vida is, yes

that's how it is, la vida ...
the great birth in the beginning,

the great death at the end
and all the small births,
small deaths, in between,
today we are all here, alive

in the sharp, dusty,
wind tasting earth between
our teeth, church bells, La Virgen, her
baby/child Jesus, towering tree sparkling

with light, the bride
and groom exit the church
fully married to the other,
the mariachi band follows

them singing they'll never be
lonely or apart in this life of
many births, many deaths, and
the old man withdraws,

having sung his gathered
song of living, tasting the
windy earth between his
teeth, this is how life is, yes.

(Three days later, my son gone.)
I step out of the
wings, the Earth shifted
on her axis half a world

away and I sing this brief
song of so many dead, "So many
births, so many deaths, we are all
human under the life/death sun ..."

The Earth's rotation accelerated,
wobbling, dancing on her axis, as

the predatory, pure white crane
walks over the exquisite lotus

eating life, giving life, this further
blossoming, our human
blossoming, the exquisite,
fleshy lotus, dust in the teeth,

yes, this is how la vida is, yes.

San Miguel de Allende
December 2004

THE SCENT OF MARIGOLDS
AND BUTTERFLIES

Señora Muerta stands holding
her muerta child tenderly in
her bony arms, flowers
perched behind each

ear, So alive, she
whispers, she laughs
the laughter of the living —
Mamacita with her little

ones, her muerto children,
her spirit children, all
around her (those that
left before their 4th

birth day) — she once
told me, eyes/voice so
tired/sorrow, "I healed
so many children, so many

people, my babies had
to pay the balance (in
Spanish, always in Spanish) —
Mamacita's altars had so

many candles, so many
dear transformed, reborn,
and as she spoke to her
21 year old son, Ruben, for

hours, listening carefully,
his replies, prayers to
La Virgen first, La Virgen
last, I remember the crushed

scent of marigolds, the
scent of wax burning, the
scent of souls (the spirits
that loved her, still visited) —

Mamacita holds her
little ones, Ruben (the unseen
ones), Lydia my mother,
Ruth my aunt, next to her,

young girls, I the tiniest
egg in Lydia's tiny, sweet,
dark womb, I smell that
moment 84 years ago as

I light the candle on
my altar; here in México
millions do the same,
the scent of crushed

marigolds in my doorway,
come in, come in,
and sparks/chispas of
my beloved dead, transformed,

reborn, begin to speak to
me, laughing, so alive;
"You will never ever die if
you remember the trail, the

scent of marigolds, the
tiniest egg in your mother's
sweet, dark womb y la
Señora Muerta cradling you

always and forever, soft
translucent butterflies fill your
mouth, sing ... sing with too
much joy, this tender life,

sing, let the soft translucent
butterflies fly free, let
each moment be your
first, your last, sing

with the taste, sing
with the scent of your
mother's tiny, tender womb,
la vida ternura, canta

y canta con mariposas
en la boca."

To the hunger, joy — Que viva....

San Miguel de Allende, México
Dia de Los Muertos, Noviembre 2005

REVISION

(El Paso, Texas)

When I crossed the
final border into the
interior, México, alone, only
small alive tornadoes
for company, I passed a freshly
made sign (did heyokas run out just for me)

REVISION

I laughed till I cried (I could hear them laughing),
as I pointed my car south, paying
tolls as I went, my solar
plexus clenching with

REVISION

my 61 year old eyes
focused like a 20 year
old (by the end of the
day, driving, they felt

their full 61), yet each
mile scraped the thinnest
film ... are they now 20,
15, 10, 5, in the womb,

I laugh, not that
easy, it's day to
night to day, the small
miracles that journey with

me like small tornadoes,
so alive, I must
remember to see, not just
look, as I'm revisioned

by the eyes of this
mysterious journey, no
destination, always
arriving with its infinite gaze.

＊

(Puerto Vallarta, México)

I saw a woman in her
80s sitting in la mar fully
clothed, her skirt billowing
out, each wave, and

with each wave she
laughed like a young
girl, her great-granddaughter
laughing with her ...

she gathered small
shells in her skirt as
her great-granddaughter ran
back to her mother, then

the entire family of women
joined her in the waves,
laughing at the young girl
this woman had become.

＊

(San Miguel de Allende, México)
Mamacita, when I threw the red
rose into your grave (me in a red
shirt), where your beautiful bones

now glow in the darkness,
my unblossomed heart vowed
to never speak Spanish ever
to anyone, my language with

you, Mamacita. Now
I must make a new
promise, a promise I've
kept, I brought your

white light spirit home,
México — México will not
be my home, the world is
my home, and I will speak

Spanish in your name, in
your Yaqui blood, Mamacita.

⚊ ⚌ ⚊

(San Miguel, my roof)

At twilight I watch
long, dancing lines of
pure, black birds flying
to El Charco, to the

lake — there's no leader,
there's no last one, as
they become one bird
mind, one bird body, one

long black
bird body
dancing, black
pearl necklace

I will
wear in
dreams,
one mind,

one body,
one long
dark dream
dancing in Earth's

last light, each
pearl at my throat,
claims my sorrow, each
bird the one great sky

song
singing
every
language,

I see.

April 2005 — December 2005

SEMANA SANTA
(HOLY WEEK)

(The Scent of Roses)

I buy a beautifully sculpted palm
frond with tiny daisies, one pink rose
tucked into it, the sweet scent of rose,
from a smiling Mexican man who could

also be Balinese, as the palm frond
could be a Balinese offering for
ceremony. I join a crowd of people, all
holding their offerings, each one slightly

different, hand made — to one side two
teams playing basketball in the morning
sun, and then I see a young, handsome
Jesus with golden lightning bolts coming

out of his head, sitting on a litter of
palms, roses, lilies, a girl of six in her
angel wings stands at his side, and
behind Jesus a group of novice priests

dressed in bright purple, blue, red,
yellow (no somber black here), each
one a striking Tibetan rocker in their
robes, their hair cut slightly punk/spiky as

they decide to be celibate for the rest of
their lives, each one a teen, early twenties.
Behind the rainbow priests, drummers,
Indian dancers, loud drums, dance

music ... this is a celebration, no sadness
here, today, no hint of the handsome, young
deity's death, the young man, Jesus — as the
Aztecs made a handsome, young man a deity,

giving him food, feminine beauty, worship, until
they cut out his sweet, beating heart, the transformation.
The young priests smile, the drums begin, the
dancers to leap, the girl angel slowly follows,

her serious, six-year-old face, follows Jesus on
his lovely litter, her mother close behindand
the mother of Jesus ... Mary, ancient Goddess,
skulls strung on her waist, snakes twining round

her arms, eagle wings spread, so many ancient
Goddesses, here I'll remember Ixchel the Maya,
before the Aztecs, the slaughter of sacrifice, the
sweet beating heart, blood of living sacrifice, the

Maya Ixchel, healer, midwife to blood of living
birth (that blood ceremony), consort to Quetzalcoatl,
handsome, beautiful God of masculine/feminine,
life/death, light/dark, who burns as the Morning

Star, his twin sister/self, Venus, sunset star.
I'm pulled into the procession by an older
woman, we walk slowly to the plazadrummers,
dancers, rainbow priests, lighting

bolt Jesus, his guardian angel (white, gauzy,
sparkling glitter-gold wings, her little girl
smile), the people begin to sing, holding
their palm offerings up, I join them as

best I can, words of gratitude, sadness,
always wonder — and as we pass under purple/white
streamers stretched house to house over cobbled
streets, petals begin to rain ... roses, lilies,

roses ... the young priests are beautiful in
roses, their hair, their rainbow robes, all of us in
roses, lilies, roses, smiling women rain petals of
roses, lilies, roses, over us all, tears sting

my eyes, as I feel my grandmother's soft so
soft hand in mine, and though I hear her begin to
sing so softly, so sweetly, I don't gaze at her covered in
roses (I don't want her to go away, not yet), covered in roses.

(Jesus On The Cross, Jesus OFF The Cross)
I don't watch the so-called Passion Play, the
crucifixion, at the main plaza — I don't watch
the men whipping themselves with small

ropes, self flagellation, but I
do buy one for bad guests, hang it
in my kitchen, cheerful, bright colors of
white/red/purple — maybe next year I'll brave

it, maybe next year I'll kidnap the young,
handsome Jesus, set him free to the
beautiful, young Mexican women that
parade in the plaza (as I did with my

visiting son, I turned him over to the
women at 3 am, took a taxi home). In my
favorite church, run only by nuns, there's no
suffering Jesus on the altar, he's intact and

smiling — a small altar to El Niño Doctorcito with
those golden lightning bolts on his head, his
tiny doctor bag in one hand, surrounded by
small trucks, his toys — I always drop

some pesos on his altar, La Virgen's altar,
brown skinned, surrounded by roses, Ixchel
in this guise, ancient mother/daughter/lover/healer,
surrounded always by her roses, as the rain of

roses, lilies, roses fell on us all.
Instead, I go to my first bull fight, bull
fights, a ten-year-old matador, a young
blonde huera woman, handsome young

man on horseback, two men matadorsthis
is the Passion Play, this is the safe
crucifixion of the Other, the one who must
die that we may live — each bull is pierced, tortured,

bled, each bull is confused, thirsty, in pain. And then,
one dies suddenly, just dies, no sword, no bravery, the
ten-year-old matador is trampled, tossed, whisked
out of the ring to sad macho cheers ...

You are the son I never had,
you are the self I never had,
you are the killer, not the martyr ...
fresh bull in the ring, he takes the

cape out of the matador's trembling
hands. TORO TORO TORO the crowd
cheers, I cheer QUE VIVA EL TORO
and the very handsome, very slick, young

drug lords next to me join in, laughing,
I sip their Sangre de Toro vino, two more bulls
take the cape from los matadors, TORO
TORO TORO, the gorgeous (middle name Hermoso,

Beautiful) young horseman on his pure, white horse,
kills the bull, tossing his ear almost into my lap, and
the crowd continues TORO TORO TORO QUE VIVA
EL TORO, the young dazzling drug lords texting, sending

photos, talking in low voices on their cells, turning to
smile at me provocatively, the age of my youngest
son, my granddaughter — I'm whacky but not that
whacky, I smile back, they pour me more

Sangre de Toro, I sip. Later, I buy a
picador, a colorful glittering spear from a
hawker, a stylized twin of the one that
tortured the bulls, a real raw metal point

(if the still un-caught serial rapist enters, he's
dead). Later, I go with friends to an art
opening held in an architect's home, immense
cactus on the roof, if you trip you're in trouble, chaos

of thorns, long silver spears. I laugh and order a huge free
tequila with slices of lime, flirt with a painter, then
go sit in the solitude of full moon light, crickets
dancing the air — I think of the young drug lord's

dangerous beauty, I sigh, I smile, put down my
colorful glittering picador, and I hope the poor,
the needy, eat the flesh of fresh bull tonight. The
Other dies that we may live.

(The Presence of Joy)

Almost daily, pre-dawn fireworks
jolt me from dreams, the softening
sky fills with orgasms of color,
pulling me to my roof, mouth open

I watch — who knows the sacred
day, the saint, the reason, the
sky is filled with multiple orgasms,
raining rainbows of fire, the violet sky

is filled with the presence of joy
softly falling to Earth, softly raining to
Earth, raining, reaching us humans, some
so poor they sit on the cobble streets wordlessly

begging with their children, some breast feeding
a baby (these are the Indians), many are ancient
grandmothers, blind grandfathers (I stop with
pesos, pan dulce, the grandmothers bless me) —

some going to work in the pre-dawn light,
large groups of people ... the waiters, maids,
janitors, diggers of ditches, car washers
who work for (if they're lucky) 200 pesos a day,

20 usd, the middle class in their SUVs,
the upper class being driven who knows where,
but the joy is for every one as it softly, so softly,
falls to Earth — the middle/upper class

may stop in their day to place pesos in a hand, the
poor will accept, blessing them (each one gives
what they have). I wake from a dream speaking
Spanish in the dream, I realize, as the

presence of joy falls softly, rains fire to
the Earth and I force myself to run, to
run to the roof facing houses, people,
ringed by these mountains, immense flocks

of birds winging fire — "Joy is
the only thing that makes life bearable,
blessing us," I murmur.

(The Element of Ecstasy)

I sit on the roof at midnight, half moon
over my head, I throw my head back in the
cooling breeze to watch the shimmering half
moon ... in that moment, gliding pure white crane
marries light.

La Casa Orizaba, México
April 2006

THE CHILD
(Dragon)

I'm trying not to write the first
line of my novel, if I do
I'm doomed, I can't stop until
the last line is written, the very

last line is written, every character has
had her/his say, told their story, fought
with me to be free, alive, on the pageand
me, their author, writing to be free, stay

free, it's a journey, a stroll, a dance, never
ever a race to the finish, so I'm
trying not to write the first line of
my novel here in San Miguel de Allende, I'm

trying to understand the rhythm of sun, moon, stars,
the precise velocity of wind at sunrise, sun
set, the movement of clouds, birds (the other
day, a small glowing cloud turned into a child

dragon, which made me stop doing all the things
I thought I should be doing — laundry, emails,
student work I read line by line, then the
whole for their true voice, their true

vision, and the child dragon laughed as dark
thunder clouds gathered, lightning struck the
horizon, the child dragon laughed within her
sunlit cloud, lightning flashed, rain tore her

perfect beauty, but she laughed knowing a
poet/writer would tell you she existed forever,
those minutes on a warm turbulent late
August day when lightning, thunder, rain gather

daily to wash the world new in San Miguel
de Allende, the child dragon as her mouth,
her voice disappeared, but I will always
remember her perfect beauty, her playful

laughter falling to earth, such freedom to
live in the sky, loving the earth so much
you laugh as your perfect beauty becomes
more perfect, part of every living thing, every

living being, torn to pieces, becoming
whole, I will always remember her
and now so will you, don't forget her —
I'm trying not to write the first line and the
child dragon laughs).

Yesterday two young men — one with a
drum, one with a worn trumpet, came
playing up my street — a young pregnant
woman knocked on all the doors with a

plastic cup in her hand, most didn't answer,
I ran upstairs for pesos, ran back, opened
the door to her fading smile, she saw
me, her smile returned, she laughed, carrying
a new child dragon.

I stopped to talk to a man
selling photo-paintings where
the women come to wash their lives
clean by hand, I did that years ago as

a young mother, washed our lives clean
by hand — diapers, sheets, diapers — I
remember my hands becoming red until
my first wringer-washer (to walk to the

laundry in the projects was to risk our
lives) — when I told this man I refused to write
the first line of my novel, he laughed (like the
child dragon), told me he pushed his crowning

son back into his lover's birth canal thirty-one
years ago, I gasped at the pain of crowning,
having done it four times myself, as
I waited for breakfast, I pushed this poem
out.

⸻

Hurricane Juan plays with the Mexican
coastline, his ancient lover la mar, and
humans become upset, terrified (who can
blame them/us?), but this is an ancient

intimate dance between lovers,
sky/earth/la mar — the Earth wobbles,
spins on her new axis, global warming
may make us one more extinct species,

this ravishing miraculous planet (who will
witness the child dragon, who will hear her
laugh within her sunlit cloud, who). Me?
I refuse to write the first line of my novel

here in San Miguel de Allende
but I am listening,
I am watching,
I am dreaming, the
child (dragon).

México
late August 2006

DEAR WORLD,
dear Earth,
dear USA ... Mexican border,
all man-made borders

Over the border, in my
country (never my grandmother's
country), early morning,
sidewalk cafe breakfast,

Mexican kids in groups,
white/black couple,
older Jewish group,
Muslim man, sari wrapped

lovely woman, a large beautiful
Navajo man working, cleans the street,
the Pacific singing its usual song—
I love my country because it

contains so many, not the
so-called leaders who bring
us war and shame, but the
people, the people,

the people... A young Latino
glares, staring at the winter
high tide Pacific, surfers
trying to catch each waveuntil

a young Tibetan
monk comes laughing in
the high white winter
tide, holding his full

brown skirt higher, the
young Latino smiles —
I wonder at the endless
borders we humans

cross just to arrive,
just to fully arrive
at this moment, our
molecules dancing, speaking,

laughing, colliding, merging at
the borders, the borders of
our bodies ... we needn't cross
any borders, but just

stand still, let the
white swan come to
you, the world in its
eye. I love this Earth

because it contains
us all, no visible
borders (my grandmother's
Earth) — let the white swan
come.

⁘

This Lake Shrine, at the
edge of L.A., tenderly
contains Krishna, Buddha,
Jesus, Muslims, Jewsblue

Krishna plays the flute as
Buddha smiles in his silence,
the Goddess is the lake —
Shing Moo, Ixchel, Quan Yin,

Tara, Shakti, Spider Woman, Changing
Woman, Buffalo Woman, Thought
Woman, and she holds the white
swan that glides to me, and I see

the world in its eye, no
borders (my grandmother's

swan) ... each time I cross, I will
remember to hold the world in each

eye. I have
begun to see
no borders, no
man-made borders ...

let the white swan
come, and her mate
the black swan (the
universe in his eye).

Let me cross the USA
Mexican border each time,
from my home in México,
to my country Turtle Island ...

molecules dancing, singing,
laughing, colliding, merging
this world, dear World,
dear Earth (Mamacita's Earth) ...

Let the
white swan, black swan,
come, the world, the universe,
in their eyes, my dearest World.

It is time, it is time, it is time
for the people the people the people of this Earth, dear World.
Self Realization Lake Shrine (where
a portion of Gandhi's ashes are contained)

To the people dying in the crossing, the workers.

San Miguel de Allende, México, to
Los Angeles, Califas, and back ...
December 2006

YOUR LIFE

I remember you, you were born
two months early, just to
be born on Martin Luther King's
birth day, the unicorn I bought

to keep you company, exactly
your size, his golden horn grazing
your tiny head (after the
incubator), the hours I sat

holding you, massaging your tiny star
self, murmuring, "Stay, stay, this
Earth is so beautiful, stay, stay ..."
And you did, you stayed, now

6 foot 2, 23 years old, writer and lover of
the world, daily surfer — remember
the time in Santa Cruz, you were 17,
someone chomped by a shark at

The Point (your favorite spot to
surf), in the morning, that
afternoon you and your friends
suited up to surf The Point,

"Are you all insane?" I could see
the shark waiting for the new menu,
gliding through the waves, always
hungry. Your friends went silent,

you turned and said, "Mom, that's
where the sharks live, the ocean,"
in such a patient tone (parent to
child, almost). I snuck out with

my binoculars, waiting for The Fin, to
call 9-1-1, the shark moved on to the
great, wild ocean, as you moved on
to the great, wild world. Your life.

*To my son, Jules Villanueva-Castaño,
on his birth day, January 15, 2004.
As always, I love you more, tu madre.*

RAINBOW TEACHER

The black butterfly with
rainbow eyes, wings, comes
to claim you in The Place of
The Four Winds — you try

swatting it, laughing as it
sweeps your head, telling
you, "I am here, wandering
one, young man, sweet

teacher, I am here to teach
you your path, why
you came to the place of
your ancestors, and then

you will pass it on to so
many others. I am your sweet
Rainbow Teacher, the sacred,
rare, immense black butterfly,

I flavor your dreams,
bring you the future, always
now, sweet teacher, always
now. I was with you at

your birth, I hovered over
your mother's womb as
you pushed to breathe,
I will be there with

you, your final breath, as
you spread your rainbow wings,
open your rainbow eyes,
in The Place of The Four Winds,

always in The Place of The Four Winds,
sweet teacher, spread your rainbow wings,
open your rainbow eyes — now.

A mi hijo, Jules Villanueva-Castaño,
El Charco, Los Quatro Vientos,
San Miguel de Allende, México,
October 2005

A MI HIJO, JULIO
(To My Son, Jules)

Don't forget the young
man singing by the house,
"Miel, compra compra miel,"
the sunlit honey perched

in his hands to tempt the
eye, to tempt the
tongue — as I bought
miel, honey, he showed me

the deep, red mark from
the strap on his shoulder,
"Ayyyy," I murmured, "Si,
es duro ... Yes, it's hard," he

smiled the patience of an
80 year old man, maybe 18,
I bought one more. Don't forget
the 16 year olds sitting on

curbs, heads in open palms,
no jobs, no future, no hope
at 16, 17, 18, 19 ... if they
find some hope, they'll start

washing cars for 30 pesos,
2.50 usd, I always tip them
20 pesos more just to see
that light, of hope, the young

man's eyes. Don't forget
the young men digging
ditches in the Mexican sun,
maybe 200 pesos a day,

15 usd, and don't forget
your best friend, your name
sake, Julio, who lives with
his wife, three young children,

in one room, fresh plants
everywhere, his jokes, loud
laughter, muy loco dread
locks (we told him we'd

have a funeral for if he
ever cut them, we both
love his dreads), a man as
tall as you, 6 foot 2, los

dos Julios, I laughed
as you drove him home,
me in the back seat clutching
his lightning dreads, steering,

laughing, all of us laughing,
don't forget, don't forgetthe
joy in Julio's eyes as he
opened the door to his one

room cement casita, every
one he loves inside, fresh
plants, blooming cactus dreaming,
don't forget, please

don't forget
real sorrow, tears,
real joy, laughter,
in el norte, Californiayou

are the son, grandson, great,
great-great grandson of snakes and
eagles, healers, poets — fit
your joy, your love into

one unforgettable room filled with
sky, sun, moon, stars, your dreams —
I will find you in that room
in dreams. Don't forget.

A Los Dos Julios
y mi hijo, Jules, in his 25th year
San Miguel de Allende, 2006

EARTH AND SKY

You ask me what I think of
your 36 year old tiny wrinkles from
backpacking, rock climbing, snow boarding,
surfing, making love to Earth and Sky —

You ask me what I think of your
shaved-head, balding-head — you
were born without much hair, white
down, beautiful then, beautiful now —

You ask me what it feels like to see
my children grow old — I look into
your piercing, laughing blue eyes,
what I see is play, joy, wisdom,

finally wisdom, the kind you had as
a solemn, playful, joyful 2 year old
baby monkey, when you told me, "Wake up
to your mind" (you really did), and I did.

I ask you: What's it like to see
your mother grow and change from
21 to 60 — but then, I think
I know the answer because you and

I still play, I make fun of you,
you make fun of me, and I still get
you in a headlock — we are older, more
joy, more wisdom, loving Earth and Sky,

each other, each year, more
unconditionally, human to human,
son to mother. I have known
you may life times, each

time I know you better, each
time you know me better — birth
to death to birth, we play
between Earth and Sky.

To my son, Marc Jason Goulet
December 2003

BEAUTIFUL WARRIOR LIZARD
IN THE SUN

You climb the rocks in the
peaceful pool of sacred
water and cannon ball as
you did as a boy, laughing

as you emerge, so alive,
I laugh with you, fighting
my instinct to pretend I don't
know you, never seen this

guy in my life, you
climb the rocks to leap
once more, I disappear into
the dark tunnel, into

the grotto, la gruta, where tangible
light lives, the Mexican people hold
out their open hands to catch it for a
moment, la luz, so clear, so alive (in the

darkness, sun's light), it blesses you.
I hear your huge splash, smile at a
38 year old man whose boy makes
him leap — soon you'll join me, hold

out your hand to catch la
luz for a moment, and
when it blesses you, you'll
laugh and I'll join you —

I'll curb my desire to climb the
rocks, whoop as I cannon
ball (the way I dive in my
mountains, screaming, my

eagles always come, soaring,
singing their eagle song).
You are the son who built the
small platform at the tip of the

highest tree by our cabin in the
Sierras (you were so brave at
14, getting most of our winter
wood, the man-sized chain saw;

you still are, brave). And so,
as we leave the hot springs,
an immense, beautiful lizard
perches on a cactus just for

you — I've never seen one this large,
this beautiful, this brave,
how it perches without
fear just for you, just for

you. I remember the first
time I climbed up to the
perch, the tallest pine, how
it swayed in the wind, how

the smell of fresh resin filled my
eyes, nose, mouth, joy, how
a swift falcon grazed my
head, my soul flying out,

laughing, it soared, how
you looked up and laughed,
leaving me alone to hear the
wind, her song, my words.

How we've always honored
fearlessness in the other — you
are the son I remember then,
you are the son I remember now,

and this beautiful
brave warrior lizard
is just for you,
just for you, Marco.

To my son, Marc Jason Goulet
La Gruta, August 2005
San Miguel de Allende, México

DEAR WORLD,
dear Earth,
April 29, 2008

Food prices rise world
wide, the cost of
growing it, producing it,
manufacturing it,

marketing it,
distributing it,
advertising it,
presenting it,

the poor world wide
begin to starve in
larger numbers, the
poor in the USA,

the richest country on
Earth, go hungry
daily — billions in debt,
the Holy War For Oil,

the price of oil so
high, the manufacture of
food so high, the poor
begin to starve —

I hear someone singing,
"Fresa ... fresa ... fresa,"
open my door, an
older man selling ripe

strawberries — I bring him
water, this hot day, the
cobbled streets, "Gracias,"
he smiles — I pay him

25 pesos for my two bags of
red ripeness. A teen knocks,
fresh warm tortillas, a
man with his cart of hot

ears of corn, peeled mangoes,
pineapples, fresh juices, a
woman knocks with her
still-warm tamales wrapped

in foil, a man carrying
flowers in a bucket, high
on his shoulders, an old
man, his wife, knock, their

burro laden with fresh
vegetables, calla lilies
and roses, the ice cream
truck's music tempts

me, the neighborhood kids,
the richest home-made ice
cream on a cone for
6 pesos — the milk

truck at 7 pm daily,
the teen pours fresh
milk from the farm
into neighbor's containers,

everyone smiling, joking,
fresh milk, 10 pesos for a
bucket — and the street
stands that line my street,

fresh home-made food, more
than I can eat for 30 pesos,
including the drinks. I won't
even describe the markets,

rainbows of vegetables,
fruits, trucked by families
to sell, chickens roasted
whole, freshly killed

meat from the ranches
wait to be inspected, bought,
fajitas, tacos, enchiladas ...
and the flower stands make

make me dizzy with beauty,
the vendor offering me his
queens, as he calls them,
roses, and I buy two

dozen for 40 pesos, he
adds other flowers, his
gift.
Dear World,

Dear Earth,
May everyone on this planet,
our home, eat as I do in
San Miguel de Allende, México,

and may they buy
roses from a man
who calls them his
queens.

DEAR WORLD,
dear Ixchel*
May 10, 2008

We learn, the one
hundred monkeys — the
first one drops a
coconut, it cracks
open, accident — the second
an accident, until the
100th monkey, thousands of
miles away drops the coconut

on purpose, open, we
learn, evolution.
Malcolm X surrounded by
a so-called panel on TV,
red-faced white men,
their rude crude mean
spirited questions, and he,
Malcolm X, sits there

among them, centered,
peaceful, powerful, flowing,
so much youthful energy,
beauty, African prince, his
very presence challenges
them, provokes them to
anger, resentment, violence
in their gaze — Malcolm X

centered, peaceful, powerful,
flowing, beauty, African
prince — 43 years ago we
were still the 52nd monkey,
not yet, not yet, not
yet. King giving his sermon,
Vietnam War, the world in
his gaze, centered, peaceful,

powerful, flowing, wise,
beautiful African king,
American king, Earth king,
he spoke for all people, but
we were only on the
74th monkey, not yet, not
yet. I watch Barack Obama
surrounded by cheering black,

brown, white people,
a white father hands his
baby son to him, to hold, he
smiles to every race,
every human being, dear
World, beautiful prince,
centered, peaceful, powerful,
flowing, compassionate, wise, may

we become the 100th
monkey, may we evolve, all
human beings, may the
beautiful prince lead us,
may we lead him,
into the next phase,
the precarious, so
promising, the promise,

tipping point. May we
all become the 100th
monkey, it's time, it's
time (keep him safe,

dear Ixchel).

* Ixchel is the Mayan Goddess of transformation, healing.

RED ROSES
6:30 in the evening

The first bull, Mexican
matador, the overweight
lancers on horseback
pierce el toro's spinal

column deeply, over
and over, taking his strength,
his power, bringing him to
his knees after two half

hearted passes with the
cape, just wanting to
die — TORO TORO
TORO TORO we scream,

enraged by this cowardice of
lancers, simpering matador —
MATALO we yell,
KILL HIM, el

toro on his knees
begging for death — an older
man yells to the young, Mexican
matador, "Sin pasión te haces viejo ...

Without passion, you become old!"
We BOOOO the coward, his
dragging red cape, out
of the ring, the circle

where death came as
sword, metal, thrust,
el toro suffering, bleeding,
families of the poor will

eat tonight, the best cuts for the
rich. The second bull claims the
ring, chasing junior bullfighters with
fuchsia capes behind wooden

barricades, full of power, death
laughing at the tips of his twin
horns — the smug lancers enter,
lances poised to take his

power, we go wild
BOOOO BOOOO
Only one superfical thrust,
someone signals as we

BOOOOOOOO
confused, they leave the
circle as we stand to
cheer TORO TORO TORO

The Spaniard strolls in with power
and grace, his red cape held at hip
level, he faces el toro, an equal, respect
in his bearing, and they begin to

dance, and they begin to dance
an ancient dance of hunter/prey,
prey/hunter, death to death, and
in the last light, the great sun

showers light and shadow equally,
the circle where they dance, toro,
matador, death joins this graceful
dance of equals, twin

horns skimming the Spaniard's
slim body, so intimately,
death is his lover, his
mother, those powerful twin

horns, and el toro
knows this, we can
see that he knows
this, as he gives himself

(his immense strength,
power) to the dance of
equals, each one could
die, yet each one dances

so gracefully, so intimately,
horn to hip, horn to groin,
sword in hand, sweeping
the red cape, human and

bull breathe the same
sky, feel the fading sun's
light, shadow of moon,
equally, they dance

as we shout OLÉ
endlessly, they dance,
equals in death, in
love, they dance. The

Spaniard rises on his
tip-toes, every muscle
visible, tense, his suit
of lights sparkling at

at 6:30 in the evening, sword
drawn, ready, as his lover
passes so intimately, twin
horns caressing his thighs,

el toro passes beautifully, dancing,
death finds him dancing,
swift death, no suffering,
dancing — his lover's tender

ear in his raised hand, he
circles the ring, holding it
tenderly, not a prize, tenderly,
someone throws him una bota de

vino, he gulps as the crowd
counts UNO DOS TRES
to twelve, he drinks at 6:30
in the evening, smiling,

shouting GRACIAS as the
moon swallows the circle,
as el toro is butchered for
hunger. I want to

dance with my death
gracefully, equals, at
6:30 in the evening, the
hour of my birth, as

Venus rises spilling her
erotic light, vowing to
meet the great Sun at
dawn, facing Moon and

shadow, I want to dance
with el toro, my lover, so
intimately, human, bull,
light, dark, life, death,

those twin horns, swiftly.
Next time I'll bring red
roses for the circle, if
such a dance is dancedor

I will scatter them as
I walk, petal by petal by
blood-red petal, these
roses

are to honor
light and shadow,
bull and human,
the dance, equally,

at 6:30
in the
evening, as
Venus rises

spilling her
erotic light
on us all
equally.

To the Spaniard, Antonio Gaspar.
San Miguel de Allende, México
December 31, 2007

TWENTY SCORPIONS
(y un sueño)

I've killed at least 20 or so
scorpions, so primal, pre
historic, they live in my house in
San Miguel de Allende, my 88 year

old neighbor laughed, telling me in
Spanish, "If you don't kill your
scorpions, all of ours will come
to live with you, they build their

nests where it's warm and safe," he
laughed again. So, I took off my
flip-flop, slowly approached, it
didn't even budge, scamper, nada, it

squished — I cleaned off my flip-flop,
shuddered, they can't kill you but
they do sting. Maybe like the famous
painter at Ghost Ranch, I can collect

scorpion bodies (she collected rattles
when she killed them with her walking
stick), maybe I can put notches on
my wall, see if they go floor to ceiling,

maybe each scorpion whispers its
ancient wisdom as I kill
it, maybe what I'm really doing
is gathering/hunting wisdom.

Scorpion #1 ... The wisdom of dying.

Scorpion #2 ... The wisdom of dying without
fear.

Scorpion #3 ... The wisdom of dying with fear.

Scorpion #4 ... The wisdom of dying with joy.

Scorpion #5 ... The wisdom of dying with sorrow.

Scorpion #6 ... The wisdom of dying alone.

Scorpion #7 ... The wisdom of dying all one.

Scorpion #8 ... The wisdom of dying on a wall.

Scorpion #9 ... The wisdom of dying with no walls.

Scorpion #10 ... The wisdom of leaving the body behind.

Scorpion #11 ... The wisdom of being born.

Scorpion #12 ... The wisdom of being born from a womb.

Scorpion #13 ... The wisdom of being born from light.

Scorpion #14 ... The wisdom of being born at sunrise.

Scorpion #15 ... The wisdom of being born at midnight.

Scorpion #16 ... The wisdom of being born on Earth.

Scorpion #17 ... The wisdom of being born in the Void.

Scorpion #18 ... The wisdom of never being born.

Scorpion #19 ... The wisdom of never dying.

Scorpion #20 ... The wisdom of hunting each living scorpion, each living dream.

In my 62nd year, I am gathering wisdom
at last,
I am learning how to die in order to be
born, that

I may see
I was never ever
born, and that I
will never ever die —

this body, this human,
this woman, this scorpion
that I kill, this slow gathering,
hunting of this wisdom. This dream.

(Un Sueno)
I begin to dream in Spanish,
surprising myself as I speak
like the surprise I feel when
I kill a scorpion.

June 2006

MEMORY
Stone and Wings

Xochiquetzal, Mother Goddess of
love, born from
volcano fire, lava,
rock, I face you,

your implacable face
of love — love is
not sweet, love is
not simply charm,

chemistry, lust — I see
it in your searing
gaze, the fearlessness of
your stare, those

centuries-ancient eyes
that survive, the volcano
fire, lava, rock, the
fire of love, these

centuries past, your
children still kiss,
embrace in Oaxaca's
zocalo — this was

no easy task, the
intent you've passed
on to your children,
and to me, the ancient

instinct to trust
the softness, the
center of softness, in
the other, to surrender

the flesh, blood,
bone, to fire and
lava, the implacable
stare that whispers,

"Love is not sweet,
love is not simply
charm, chemistry, lust, love
is what survives

in the zocalo, in
the first embrace of
every lover, the memory
that creates your

wings at last."
My wings that opened
at six, choosing to
stay in flesh and

blood, lovers, children,
all my words on the
loving skin of trees,
each one cut down,

their green-veined leaves,
each one a page of
poetry, the story, the
novel. The gift of

memory, the gift of
wings, the tattoo draws
blood, fine points of
lava pain — Xochiquetzal,

you would flay me,
why not, me with my
score of loss and
gain — flay me, Mother

Goddess, tattoo my
words on my fearful,
trembling, loving
skin, remember

my wings,
make them beautiful,
make me beautiful,
once again, draw blood.

My first memory of
wings was of falling,
not wanting to wake
up, not wanting to

return to flesh, to
blood and bone, but
a great desire to eat
the sky, return to

ancient star home galaxy —
I've opened my spirit wings
only in dreams, then
words, love. Memory. Oh

my Oaxaca wings of
violet purple, open
wide to the implacable
stare of Xochiquetzal's intent,

her harsh, tender, true
vision, what creates
us, what flays
us, what remembers

us thousands of years
new, the first embrace,
the first kiss, wound,
heal, wound, heal, pain

and pleasure, pleasure
and pain, love's
harsh, tender, enduring
memory — stone and wings.

Oh my bloody
Oaxaca wings of
violet purple, tattoo,
temporary body, home, memory,

thousands of
years, always new,
this ancient, implacable
love burns. In me.

Gracias a la vida.

Birth day wings, Monte Alban
Oaxaca, México
October 2008

DIAMONDS

To let you know,
so you don't forget,
what a gift your
tears were to me,

a grown man's tears,
give them to your
wife someday, she
will treasure them,

believe me, she
will treasure them,
your sorrow and
your strength, an

equal gift, she
will hold them in
her womb like diamonds,
as she'll hold your

children like diamonds,
and your gift reminds
me how I've missed,
deeply, in my soul,

mi alma, miss the
gift of a grown
man's tears, the equal
gift of a grown

man's sorrow and
strength, you are the
first grown man to
give this to me, and now

you've shown me what
I want, at last, a man
strong enough
to weep,

that gift of
perfect diamonds
from his soul,
an equal.

To my son, Jules.
Written while eating beautiful food
in Como Agua Pa' Chocolate,
Oaxaca, July 2009, Guelaguetza

LOVE'S LAUGHTER

When you told me, after
41 years, you remembered after
41 years, your father touched
you in the bath tub at

four — I felt like a woman
in Bosnia watching her
daughter being raped, after
she was gang-raped —

I felt like a woman
in Rwanda watching her
children, every one, killed
in front of her, saving

her for months of rape in
her own home, the blood
of her children every where,
staining her fingers, her eyes,

her soul — how did this
woman survive, I wonder —
I felt like the woman
in Tibet whose son is being

tortured for his gentleness,
all the young monks in
March 2008, the brutal
Chinese leaders — I felt

like the women whose
children are forced to cut
off their hands, and the child
who must cut off their mother's

hands — how would they
survive, I wonder — an old
student interviewed the
woman kept for months, in

her own home for rape, the
blood of her children comforting
her — the woman's photo, sweet
smile of strength, peace,

strength, thick knife scars
at her throat, her direct
gaze, a smear of
blood in her left

eye, she will always
remember, she will always
hear each child's voice,
laughter — love will

survive, love
will survive,
love will
survive,

in spite of
that smear of
blood in our
left eye,

if we can remember,
if we can see,
if we can hear
love's laughter.

July 2008, México

BRUJA

"Luna, luna ..." my big
fat uncle from México
sang to me, warned
me he was looking for

me when I was five,
San Francisco, his older
sister's house, my grandmother —
"... come la tuna ..." grab

my five year old body,
"... hecha la cascara ..." hold
me squirming to escape,
"... y come la tuna!" —

tickle me till I screamed
and cried. "Leave her, what's
wrong with you, can't you
see it's no game for

her, Dios mio," take me
from his grasp. "Luna,
luna ..." I heard him coming,
searching for me, his

lumbering bulk, "... come la
tuna ..." I ran for my secret
tent under the table
cloth, my crayons and

paper waiting, "... hecha la
cascara ..." I grabbed my
blunt baby scissors, stabbed
his big fat hand reaching

for me — no "... come la
tuna!" No tickling till
I screamed and cried,
blood, I ran for

my grandmother, hid behind
her full skirt — "Give her to
me, look at my hand!"
"I told you to leave her, not

to touch her, pendejo, no."
"She'll be a bruja like
you, just like you!" She
held me close, feeling her

body tremble with laughter, he
never ever touched me,
reached for me, caution
and anger in his eyes, and

I was glad to be
exactly like her, yet becoming
only myself years later, but
she created me. That day.

When I was five
years old and
fought back,
drawing blood.

"Luna, luna," I sing
when I draw blood,
"come la tuna," I laugh
with pleasure, the escape

"hecha la casacra,"
I fight back and
I choose to love, be touched,
gracias gracias y gracias

to the strength of
the woman, la bruja,
ancestor, grandmother of
my soul, spirit, "y come la

tuna!" I eat the
sweet fig slowly,
sensually, gathering it on
my tongue, laughing —

I eat
the sweet
fig slowly,
sensually,

laughing,
"Luna, luna,
come la tuna,
hecha la cascara

y come
la tuna,
luna, luna,"*
laughing.

San Miguel de Allende,
México — March 2008

* "Moon, moon, / eat the fig, / peel the husk, naked, /
and eat the fig!"

CHANGING WOMAN
The Girl

I've been hypnotized
and analyzed
and idolized
and sanitized

and I'm still here —

I've been fantasized
and criticized
and vandalized
and marginalized

and I'm still here —

I've been cared for
and cheered for
and threatened for
and spoken for

and I'm still here —

I've been lied to
and cried to
and laughed to
and forgotten to

and I'm still here —

I've been danced with
and fucked with
and loved with
and betrayed with

and I'm still here —

I'm the strongest woman
you'll ever meet —
I'm the softest woman
you'll ever meet —

I'm the wisest woman
you'll ever meet —
I'm the biggest fool
you'll ever meet —

I'm the one with courage
to spare —
I'm the one with fear
to share —

All of me in a crazy
balance,
all of me in a sane
imbalance —

I want my Windhorse,
color of the night
and dreams,
I want the lightning

to remember my name (Sudden
Rainbow) over and over, to
bring me to the place
I am always born,

always made new, (Sudden
where the Sun is birthed
daily, her vulva — where
I become the girl seeking

only wonder, where (Rainbow
only wonder is her mother,
father, child, sister, brother,
secret lover, every (Sudden

star sings, We're still
here, the diamond
wonder, perfect perfect
wonder, always here —

The girl
I become
this wonder
Changing Woman.

    (Sudden Rainbow)

San Miguel de Allende, México
January 2008

* Changing Woman is the Navajo Goddess, who walks to the horizon
when she's tired and old, about to give up — to become The Girl, the
child, once again.

II.

BUDDHA

BUDDHA
(Dream)

Pointing at your own heart you find Buddha.
—Buddhist saying

In a car with the Buddha,
him driving, we're joking,
laughing, he misses a
curve, we fly into
sky, simply flyas
we fall fly
fall, I wonder
why I'm not afraid,
why I'm enjoying
every moment we
fly to our deaths,
we watch the sky
with gratitude, joy,
a flying being saves
us, we love that
too, the Buddha and
I, this journey
through sky and
earth, I love
each moment, fearless,
the Buddha
and I
laugh and
laugh.

San Miguel de Allende, México, 2007

SHAKTI ... GODDESS AT LARGE
(bumper sticker, San Miguel de Allende)

Whoever finds love beneath hurt
and grief disappears into emptiness
with a thousand new disguises. —Rumi

Every night, my body
on fire at 4 a.m.
as I finish this novel,
these characters who teach

me to love without
fear, burning through their
fear to love the other,
and I wonder, am I that

brave, and where the hell
is my Shakti-man, my
lover, not husband, simply
lover, I wait for my

lover at 4am, burning,
words for the novel,
whispered so clearly,
I rise to write down —

"A rapture of wings,"
the hummingbird wings
in my novel, in my life,
tiny Goddess, tiny Shakti.

— ·—·

Where will I go next ...
Shakti will show me
visions, she always
does, I follow her

footprints to wander
always, she guides me,
laughing, she guides me,
weeping, she guides me,

singing, she guides me,
dancing, as I disappear
into a thousand new
births, new cells,

new bones, new blood,
new tissue, new womb,
new eyes, new ears,
new mouth, new hands,

new feet, oh my new feet,
new birth canal (orgasms),
new body on loan,
I am ready, oh so

willing, to dream new
dreams, to see new
visions, to hear new
words, to love as

though for the first
time (I let go of
grief, transparent spores
in the wind), I forget to

weep, I will re
member, I am a
child with my brand
new heart, in the

ancient body, memory,
deep delight and joy,
1,000 births, 1,000 deaths,
Shakti, Goddess at large,

Shakti wandering the
world, in love with the
world, in love with the
Beloved, my first

love, all loves, every
love I've known was the
Beloved, is the Beloved,
my brand new womb fills

with love,
my brand new heart fills
with love,
one thousand new lives,

this loving, as the
Beloved tenderly holds
me, letting me go to the
wind, spores, wings,

in the ancient, always
new, body of Shakti,
the Goddess at large,
I follow, I am,

the Beloved, lets me go
to the wind so
tenderly, I am
loved, and I love,

I follow, I dream,
I am, 1,000 deaths,
1,000 births, 1,000 lives,
1,000 loves, this journey,

a rapture
of wings,
take to the
empty sky.

I crouch in darkness,
the roots of darkness,
the womb of darkness,
fertile, potent, oh darkness,

I dream of children,
flesh and blood,
I dream of children,
words, songs, stories,

I dream the Cosmos
birthing, dying, stars, black
holes, spirals of pulsing
light, my words, songs,

stories, are more my
self, more than my
self, I may love my
flesh and blood children

more, but I live,
I live in
the root
of creation.

I surround my self with
my books, more than
my self, I let my flesh
and blood children go

into life, to become them
selves, more than
my self, I celebrate this,
I grieve this,

I know this,
we are all at
large in the
Cosmos,

creation   creator
and I return always
return to the
root of creation

(where a 1,000 new
disguises wait, my
self, more than my
self), the Beloved,

a rapture
of wings
take to the
empty sky.

⸺ ❈ ⸺

I follow Shakti
dancing,
I follow Shakti
singing,

I follow Shakti
grieving,
I follow Shakti,
bliss,

don't ask me why,
bliss,
I can't explain,
bliss,

because I love,
bliss,
because I fight,
bliss,

because I forget,
bliss,
because I remember,
bliss,

because I let go,
bliss,
because I hold on,
bliss,

because I'm still,
bliss,
because I spin,
bliss,

because I'm full,
bliss,
because I'm empty,
bliss,

because oh yes,
because I surrender,
bliss oh
bliss,

I follow Shakti,
I am Shakti,
Goddess at large,
laughing weeping bliss.

⁎

I witness
the caterpillar's darkness,
beautiful darkness,
fertile womb darkness,

dissolving, surrendering
to darkness, what loved
the earth now loves
the sky, dissolved,

each cell, surrendering to
fertile womb darkness,
new cells, new wings
take to the empty

sky, dreams of
migration, sky-bliss,
root-bliss, wings
sprout, Shakti wings,

empty sky
I surrender
clouds wind instinct
earth pull instinct

ancient Shakti
ancient Shiva
ancient soul
new butterfly

bliss
I surrender
I surrender to
I surrender to this

I surrender to this ancient
I surrender to this ancient new
I surrender to this ancient new always
I surrender to this ancient new always born

wet
wings
of
bliss,

tiny hummingbird,
tiny Shakti,
I surrender to
bliss.

⚬⚬⚬

Quetzalcoatl, Morning Star, 6am,
burning through my window,
burning through my dreams,
ancient lover,

new lover, burning
through my dreams,
Quetzalcoatl, you who
will return, savior of

this continent, Hopi
Pahana, witnessing centuries
of war, genocide, human
hunger, you return

each day
for those
with eyes
to see,

for those
with hearts
to listen,
to love

the other,
the beloved
who rises,
dawn.

—————

Shakti dances, lifting
her burden of sorrow
joy anger grief joy,
her wings blurring bliss,

a rapture
of wings
take to, seize
the open sky.

San Miguel de Allende, México
August 2009

VISION

"Do you live in the
country of the blind?"
the Mexican in Los Angeles
asks me ... "You are beautiful,

I'm sure you've been
told," smiling into my
soul. "Maybe," I
laugh, blushing in the

Customs line from
USA to my home now in
México — "Do you live in
the country of the

blind?" his smile, his
question reaches me in
my secret place of
shame, longing, shame, to

simply be who
I am — I fire back,
"You are shamelessly
charming (and handsome too,

shamelessly alive, I say silently),
thank you," I laugh. "Get on your
plane, hermosa, I've seen
beauty today," you touch my

shoulder so gently, laughing,
and your words reach me in
a drought-stricken landscape
I didn't even know I had, where

the natives are starving, surrounded
by lushness, flowers, so

many flowers, fruit dripping
from laughing trees, fish

leaping onto shore offering
themselves for our
pleasure, sweet deer
pausing to greet

us, their soft
sustenance, water
so pure it
sings day and

night for-ever and
ever, the air
sky air sky
we breathe

makes us live to
150, dancing into
death transformation
death transformation, young

from first breath
to final breath, young —
I tell the starving oh
so beautiful natives, "We

now live in the country of
vision, beautiful vision,
spectrum of existence,
joy sorrow joy, we

see it all, and I see
you on the drought-stricken
earthscape
as you reach out for

ripeness, sweet sustenance,
singing water, dancing air,

singing oh singing
shamelessly, yes, shamelessly,

and I tell you, "You are
beautiful, oh so beautiful,
and you are
loved between

fertile Earth,
potent Sky,
you are
loved,

you are
loved,
now now and
now, eat drink

sing dance
love
oh love
your self

the other
no shame ...
sing with me
now oh sing

with me, I am loved
I am loved
I am beautiful
I am beautiful

I live in the country of
vision ...
You are loved
you are beautiful

welcome home oh
shameless one

with eyes to
see

the spectrum
of your beauty
of existence,
vision.

San Miguel de Allende, México
July 2008

PINU'U
(Hopi) ... "I am I"

Kokyangwuti ... Spider Woman was wise
when she took dark earth in
her hands, mixing it with
her sacred saliva, covering

the Sacred Twins, then
woman, man, in white light
substance (the creative
wisdom itself) — she

created our bodies, spirits,
minds, not our ancient souls,
she only welcomed us home, our
Grandmother, Spider Woman,

Kokyangwuti ... she was so wise, creating
sweet juicy grapes, blueberries,
blackberries, mangos, papayas,
apples, pineapples, Mother Corn

to eat — she was so wise,
creating eyes to fill with beauty,
warning, the hunt, beauty, the
ears to fill with wind,

soothing waters, predator
snapping twig, cry of
newborns and lovers, the
nose to sniff harvest,

tiny flowers, wet fur
waiting on the path, first
breath, final breath, each
breath, a gift — and the

mouth, the mouth, the
mouth to kiss the lover's
mouth, the lover's sweet
skin, the newborn's sweet

skin, the mouth and skin of
loved ones, friends, fleeting
friends, the oldest friends,
student's skin, sweet cheek,

the gratitude of teaching, being
taught, the gratitude of
loving, being loved, being
kissed, skin to skin, the

blood flowing, tiny rivers
to the ocean of the heartand
yes, the hands, yes, the
hands that obey us, to

create pleasure, pain, hold
the blood-soaked newborn,
the pale body transforming, dying,
the erect penis, the rose

petaled clitoris, vagina, womb,
the soft sac testicles,
female/male wisdom in open
hands, full breast milking,

male breast, nipple shivering
beneath my hands, slicing
vegetables, skinning chicken,
stirring curry, with my

hands, I've fed nations with my
hands, I've cradled the Cosmos, my
hands, I bring the Sun up daily, my
hands, I fix the Moon nightly, my

hands, I scatter stars throughout
the Cosmos, hot and dying, my
hands, I paint the ocean with my
hands, I sweep the Earth with

summer, fall, winter, oh spring, my
hands, I caress clouds, mountains, my
hands, my hands, my tireless human
hands — and the bony feet, who

invented them from the paw,
no fur, my naked bony feet,
they've walked, they've
run to love,

they've stood my ground, my
naked bony feet, and
they've fled from danger,
cruelty, my naked bony feet,

they've danced with drums,
flutes, so many voices, and
we've traveled to brand new,
unknown beauty, my naked bony

feet, and all of me, all my
journeys from first step to
final step, so much joy,
so much joy, yes sorrow

and grief, but my naked bony
sturdy stubborn oh so delicate
feet (and I) prefer to dance,
travel into the unknown, weeping,

laughing, always laughing, for
simple joy — "Pinu'u," Hopi,
"I am I," Tuawta, One who
sees magic, her vision, now,

my wings, Kokyangwuti,
Spider Woman, our Grandmother,
what of my wings, the ones
my grandmother coaxed into

being, unfurling in the dream,
what of my wings, invisible,
filled with light, the ancient
pollen on the wind, they

dwarf my tattooed wings perched
on my shoulders, when I fell
in my dreams at six, my grandmother
commanded, "Open your wings, now," in

Spanish — the ancient pollen
wind caresses me, a raven
laughs, a hawk hunts, and
an eagle spirals upward to

Taiowa, the Sun, oh my wings, my
wings, when I fall you open
wide, always the journey, laughing weeping,
"Pinu'u ... I am I" Tuawta, who

tirelessly hunts the magic, as
I stand in my sixty-fifth year,
such beauty, such pollen,
I fall, wings wide.

"Tienes coraje, niña, corajuda,"
my grandmother would laugh —
"You have courage, child, angry
courage." She always said

this laughing as though looking
into my future, and I always
thought coraje meant anger, till
I looked it up the other day

coraje simply means *courage*,
now I understand she blessed me
daily for my life, my daughter born
on her birth day, my fifteenth

year, three more children (coraje),
stealing food, baby clothes at fifteen (coraje),
my first published poem, story, novel (ayyy coraje),
I fall, wings wide, Pinu'u ... I am I
(mi coraje, my courage).

San Miguel de Allende, México
September 2009

NANAPWALA
(Hopi) ... "Purifiying from within oneself"

I remember the first desire,
    milk   milk   warmth—
I remember the first hands,
    soothing   holding   leaving—
I remember the first words,
    beauty   beauty   burden—
I remember the first fight,
my uncle from México tickling me till
    I screamed, wept, my grandmother
    taking me from him,
    he came searching, calling my
    name, singing, "Luna luna, come
    la tuna ..." to my secret cave,
    under the huge table cloth, his
    fat hand reaching, reaching,
    I aimed, stabbed him with
    my blunt baby scissors, drawing
blood, I remember I won
    I won   I won   I won,
my grandmother shielding me,
I remember my first fight
and how I won
my freedom —
I remember the first light, the
longing for womb darkness, the
light stinging my tender irises,
iris in Spanish *rainbow*,
I remember the first light giving
birth to the spectrum of my
vision   longing   sun   light
dreaming wandering dreaming wandering —
I remember my first song, poem,
Mamacita taught me, the way
it etched its way into my skin, blood,
bones, poetry, my mother tongue,
breath song breath poetry

I remember *Titaptawi*, my first
song poem of happiness—
I remember my first love, my first
child, a daughter, tiny goddess
born from my child body
born to earth sky earth—
my first love, child love
born to trust die trust—
always die   always trust
La Inocenta   The Innocent
who heals from her wounds
knowledge   pain   scars   healing
blood roses   red roses
always opening   the Sun—
I remember my second love,
woman's love, my third final
son from my woman's body,
born to earth sky earth,
tiny god, palm of my hand,
tiny eagle in my nest, mother eagle,
I taught him flight, my outstretched
wing (all my children, flight),
always die (fall) always trust (fly)
the song of the wind
luring you from the nest,
luring me from the nest,
hoya, Hopi ... Ready to fly
    off nest ...
I remember wings   wings   wind
the song of the four winds
La Inocenta singing
at the edge
of the world,
hoya ... .

PATUWVOTA
(Hopi) ... "Water shield, flying shield"

My grandmother told me
whenever I saw the rainbow,
tangakwunu, Hopi, I was
blessed by the Spirits, how

she lowered her head in greeting,
earth greeting, smiling to the
sky — and so tangakwunu,
rainbow, the arc that marries

Earth and Sky, always makes
me smile, laugh with joy, the
joy of a child who sat on a
small carpet for an afternoon

waiting to fly, waiting to greet
the clouds sun moon rain
bows in new lands, over
oceans, over lakes, arteries of

the Earth, glistening Sky,
I think that's when the water
shield, the flying shield, came
to me, that afternoon I waited

to fly, I flew that
night in dreams, my small
wings so shy, so brave,
small rainbows, I flew,

the water shield, arteries of
Earth, the flying shield,
oh star filled Sky, the Spirits
blessed my small tangakwunus

rainbow wings,
butterfly wings,
hummingbird wings,
raven wings,

hawk wings,
owl wings,
eagle wings, all wings,
my wings, small rainbows,

blessed by
Earth and
Sky, Patuwvota,
Tangakwunu.

HAKOMI?
(Hopi) ... "Who are you?"

First I was Hehewuti, Warrior
Mother Kachina, first — children
in my womb, words in my womb,
songs in my womb, desire in my
womb, always desire in my
womb, seeds and rivers, trees
and ocean, earth and sky,
death and desire in my womb —
I hold it all, I am empty —
"Hakomi? ... Who are you?"
I am Pahana, one of millions,
long lost mixed-blood sister,
coming home, always home, this
planet, cosmos, gazing, dreaming
Saquasohuh, Blue Star Kachina,
far away, millions of us
dream, pray, "Stay far away,"
or our continent explodes,
our planet explodes, our dreams
explode, the prophecy says,
when Blue Star Kachina dances in
the plaza our great-great-great
grandchildren's dreams will tremble,
never ever ever dance in the plaza —
"Hakomi? Who are you?"
I am a woman, mother, lover, gatherer of
words, this word kuwanlelenta, daily ...
To make beautiful surroundings ...
"Hakomi? Who are you?"
I can't be who
I was, I'm becoming who
I am.

KUWANYAUMA
(Hopi) ... "Butterfly showing beautiful wings"

Kwahu, warrior eagle, out
stretched wings within a dark
circle, my left hand, my
tattoo, my passport into
the Gateway ... pain to
pleasure, pleasure to pain,
tears to laughter, laughter to
tears, dreams to waking, waking
to dreams, life to death,
death to life, birth to
unborn, unborn to birth,
my passport to all borders, tiny
Kwahu, warrior eagle, flying
in the circle of my flesh, flying
in the sky of my flesh,
when it is time,
when it is time
my soul will join
your wings through
the Gateway
and we will be
kuwanyauma
showing our beautiful
wings.
And we
will be
kuwanyauma
showing our
beautiful wings,
Kwahu,
warrior eagle,
Kwahu.

TAWEYAH
(Hopi) ... "Magic shield"

I found taweyah years ago in
my mountains, the Sierras, tierra
de las Plumas, in a rocky place
called Spring Garden, surrounded
by forest, boulders taller than I, in
spring the tiniest wild roses on the
path to my peak, the scent of
lush, fertile, tiny wombs
lined my stony path, rattlers slid
to safety, a mountain lion growled
low in his throat, following my feet,
I sat and prayed to that growl,
then continued my path to the
peak where mountain after
mountain could be seen, mists,
clouds, eagles, my
magic shield surrounding me,
cradling me, singing to me, in
the wind, I was afraid of
no thing, only praise,
only praise
as I watched taweyah
spin, mists, clouds, eagles,
only praise.

TUWANASAVI
(Hopi) ... "Center of the Universe"

Today I'm happy for no reason, today
I dance for no
reasontoday
I sing for no
reasontoday
I breathe for no
reason —

Tuwanasavi, Center of the Universe,

this place where my two feet
stand in my sixty-fifth year, these
two feet remember baby feet, these
hands remember baby hands, this
joy remembers baby joy,
for no reason at the
Center of the Universe,
Tuwanasavi,
today I remember joy joy joy
for no reason at all joy,
Tuwanasavi,
today I remember baby laughter
in my sixty-fifth year for no reason
here
at the Center
of the Universe,
Tuwanasavi.

October 2009, birth day

TUWKSI
(Hopi) ... "Complete cycle of life"

*"That is the Sun,'" said Spider Woman. "You are meeting Taiowa,
your Father-Mother, the Creator for the first time. You must always
remember and observe these three phases of your Creation. The time of
the three lights, the dark purple, the yellow, and the red reveal in turn
the mystery, the breath of life and the warmth of love."*
—Frank Waters, *Book of The Hopi**

I.

The cycle has begun, I feel it,
I see it, kuwanyauma,
Butterfly showing beautiful wings,
my own hard-won beauty at

sixty-five, look well, you'll see
it, like beautiful butterfly
wings, a little tattered, a
little faded, but so alive,

so alive in the purple
wind, the yellow wind,
the coming red wind, as
the great Sun rises, always rises,

every newborn being,
every dying being,
pauses to greet the
great Sun, the red

wind pulsing in the east,
we breathe that red wind,
we live, we die, we are
born, this Earth, this Sky,

Mother/Father/Creator, we
are always born into
flesh, into spirit, into
tuwksi, the

man in Bali, waving me
over to buy a perfect shell,
smiling his beautiful Balinese
smile, how could I resistat

sunset on Mount Batur, volcano
home, shadow lake below, a
woman tapped my arm, holding two
carved tortoise spoons, I sighed,

taking them from her hands — the
turtle hunters on Lembongan Island,
their killing spear, their child
laughter, taking me out to snorkel,

the mysterious fish, eels, rainbows
surrounding me, the Bali Sea,
young lawyer-priest bringing
me a full glass of vodka, soda

on the side, lime sliced flowers,
I laughed, we shared the vodka
collins, the lime sliced flowers,
talking as the moon increased, the

Bali Sea moved beneath us, the
man in Baja boarding the heaving
bus, no room to sit, I holding on, sitting,
for dear life, he plants his feet

wide, brings the slung guitar in
front, begins to play and sing
of all the loves he's ever known,
so much joy, no regret in his

voice, and his glittering eyes tell
me, Let go, do not hold on to
any thing, let go, and he sings,
so much joy, people smiling, laughing,

the poor of the world accept
these simple, true gifts, and
so do I, so do I, as the young
mother next to me hands me

her toddler, smiling into my eyes,
she breast feeds the baby, the
toddler pokes my face, we laugh
as the man continues to sing of

all the loves he's ever known, so
much joy, no regrets, these
simple, true gifts — accept,
let go, accept, let go, the

gift of life, de la vida,
tuwski, Complete cycle of
life, Butterfly showing beautiful
wings, *kuwanyauma* ...

II.

SONG OF CREATION
(Hopi)

The dark purple light rises in the north,
A yellow light rises in the east.
Then we of the flowers of the earth come forth
To receive a long life of joy.

We call ourselves the Butterfly Maidens.
Both male and female make their prayers to the east.
Make the respectful sign to the Sun our Creator.
Humbly I ask my Father-Mother,

The perfect one, Taiowa, our Father-Mother,
The perfect one creating the beautiful life
Shown to us by the yellow light,
To give us perfect light at the time of the red light.

On this path of happiness, we the Butterfly Maidens
Carry out her wishes by greeting our
Father–Mother Sun.
The perfect one, Taiowa, our Father–Mother Sun.
We call ourselves the Butterfly Maidens.

KUWANLELENTA
(Hopi) ... "To make
beautiful surroundings"

Even when I was very poor as
a child of eight, when I finally
went to the store to steal food
for my grandmother and me,

curling my hands into fists, to
fight, I always brought back a
small flower for her altar and
we'd laugh as we ate the

stolen Spam, bread, jam,
milk. My grandmother's altars
were always beautiful, finding
small stones, seashells, flowers

on the way, her favorite red roses,
so when I found a flowering bush
I picked four quickly, bleeding from
shy thorns, she praised me for

their beauty — and when I
lived with my children, we
always had flowers at the center
of our table, as well as food,

the poetry my grandmother taught
me, the beauty of red roses,
the beauty of singing words,
she taught me always

to create beauty as
I go, and if you
bleed, don't cry,
laugh, at the sheer

luck of finding
perfect red roses
for free, watch
beauty

disappearing over
flowers, siyamtiwa,*
it will return soon, kissing
your open hand.

San Miguel de Allende, 2010

* Siyamtiwa — Object disappearing over flowers.

BREATHING WHILE BROWN

To the beautiful, brave
young who have always
sat at lunch counters,
racists spitting on them, pulling

their hair, calling them nigger,
killing the brave, young, white
students who joined them, the
insane dogs taking bites of their

tender skin, the insane police who
hose them down, killing pressure,
to their knees, take them to
hot filthy jails, the ones meant

for Colored — the beautiful,
young Black Panthers, Brown Berets,
hunted into extinction, AIM at
Wounded Knee, Leonard Peltier in

jail over twenty years, a wise man,
a shaman, after all these years,
knowing the spirit always, yes,
always free — Maclom X,

Mandela knew this, every pregnant
woman knows this, Gandhi
knew this, Aung San Suu Kyi
knows this, the spirit is always, yes,

always free. I remember my
youngest son followed home
daily in Santa Cruz, Califas, Breathing
While Brown, I went to the cop

station and had a fucking fit, what
do we do when an entire
state makes it perfectly legal
to punish humans for Breathing

While Brown — nine young, beautiful
brown warriors chained themselves
to the Capitol's entrance, that's what
we do, the beautiful, brave

young. Cesar Chavez would be
proud. Martin Luther king would be
proud. Ghandi would be
proud. Dolores Huerta is

proud, of the beautiful,
brave young. And my son
continues to breathe while brown,
always free.

*To my son, Jules Villanueva-Castaño, my daily
hero, works with families, kids, teens at risk.
Arizona's SB 1070, the banning of our books,
which can not ever be silenced, always free.*

San Miguel de Allende, April 2010

FIERY WOMBS

My grandmother, Jesus, full blood
Yaqui, a curandera/healer from
Sonora, who popped the paper
sack with her hand at the

border crossing, the rude
officer emptying all her carefully
packed luggage, boxes, pregnant with
my mother, crossing legally with her

minister/poet husband to a church in
East Los Angeles, she blew it up, popped
it, shouting, AIRE MEXICANA, I can
see her eagle eyes from my

childhood, defiant to her
molten core, her heart, her
spirit, her fiery womb — I read this,
that women are born with their

ovaries, all their eggs, so a part
of us in our grandmother's, great
grandmother's, great great, their
wombs, their fiery wombs,

in my daughter, my granddaughter,
my great great, yes, grandson,
my sons born from these fiery
ancestor wombs, we are.

Yesterday in line for my FM-3 to
live in México, I saw the
photo they chose, among the
smiling, friendly ones — I look

like I have indigestion, someone's
trying to fuck with me, someone
won't let me travel the ancient
trade routes, the I-don't-need-no-stickin-

badges-look, not pretty,
believe me, and I start to laugh,
"I look like a damn criminal,"
I say to the customs guy, he protests

that I don't, look like a criminal —
"I'm a border crosser, so I
must be," I laugh louder. "Ayyy
señora," he shakes his head. We

Villanueva women, Jesus Villanueva,
cross our borders with Kokopelli's
ancient flute in our ears, laughing,
shouting, dancing, fiery wombs.

Arizona's SB 1070 gives me indigestion,
QUE VIVA ...

San Miguel de Allende, May 2010

QUE PINCHE

From San Miguel to
Los Angeles, Customs waiting
for baggage — on
the Mexican plane

I had my customary
shot of free tequila,
yes, they serve you free
breakfast, juice, cerveza

y tequila, the stewardess
always laughs as she
pours me a shot at
7am, only a few men

join me as we reach
the clouds, sun
rising, the burning comfort
of tequila with breakfast

tamale, juice, cafeso
I'm feeling relaxed
till I read the sign in
Customs, $500,000 fine

for smuggling fruit, food
(whatever) across the border,
and I remember my Mexican
banana in my purse, I

forgot to eat my Mexican
banana, so I quickly pull
it out, begin stuffing
it in my mouth

"THERE IS NO EATING
OF FOOD IN THIS AREA,
PUT THE BANANA
DOWN!" Jehovah booms

over the loudspeaker, "It's
a Mexican banana," I mutter,
stuffing my entire Mexican
banana in my laughing

mouth, others begin to
giggle with me — he
rushes out, fat and
red-faced, "I could

fine you for that,
lady!" he whines
without the loud
speaker, "I told you

to put that banana
down!" "The Mexican
banana is now in neutral
territory, my stomach,"

I stare him down, fighting
not to laugh, giggles
spring up around me as
he stomps back to his god

cage, the guy next to
me says, "Que pinche,"
which says it all, and I
want a second shot of

tequila. Do they own all
the bananas on this Earth,
especially the Mexican
bananas I see in the

supermarkets USA,
do they own my eyes,
my hands, my feet, my
laughing mouth, and do

they even own my stomach,
my heart, my sweet womb that
my Yaqui Mexican grandmother
gave me, the fertile

womb that she gave
me, the defiant womb
that she gave me — all I
can say is,

after my second
shot of
tequila,
"Que pinche."

(DISFRUTE)
San Miguel de Allende,
in the huge mercado,
market, vege vendors

wield their swords, slicing
papaya, mango, watermelon,
fat strawberries for you,
"DISFRUTE," they laugh,

"TASTE THIS, ENJOY THIS,"
shoving it into your
hands, heavy, ripe, wet,
so delicious, sensual,

alive with pleasure Mexican
fruit, veges, no one
claiming dominion over
your eyes, hands, feet, laughing

mouth, heart, sweet womb,
your curious, hungry stomach,
DISFRUTE, TASTE THIS,
ENJOY THIS, and I do, I do.

In the modern Mega supermarket
it's become a mercado, freshly
cooked food, piles of
tempting vegetables, fruit,

a pig's head decorated
with daisies, surrounded by
pastries, I've stopped
asking, Why this combo, I

just enjoy the beauty, the
chaos, DISFRUTE, people
leap and smile to
serve me red rice with veges,

block of quivering flan, stewed
broccoli, cauliflower, carrots
con cilantro, fresh red, green
salsas with chunks of

tomatoes, jalapenos floating,
piles of cobalt blue
tortillas, still warm
in their wrappings —

I'm so happy I don't
need a shot of tequila
(though I wouldn't pass
it up), and a young

woman has sample
plastic cups of the
best, hey it's 10am,
it is the best, she

smiles DISFRUTE, the
first time I saw
this I was tempted to
speed dial '911,' just

moved here, in the wide
vege, fruit area, right in
the center, a butcher's block
with an immense machete,

gleaming and wet, I watched
a woman pick a perfect
papaya, bring it to
the butcher block, the

gleaming machete, she
gently, so lovingly,
sliced it open,
revealing its endless

rows of black-seed
glistening children that
taste like pepper compared to
their mother's sweet womb flesh —

I walked over, picked a
perfect, green, ripe watermelon,
to the butcher block, people
actually stopped to watch,

sensing my virgin journey of
the gleaming, wet machete,
I balanced it with my left
hand and gently, so lovingly,

sliced, revealing her sweet,
juicy, red womb, her tiny,
hard, black-seed children,
and I stole a slim slice,

and people smiled DISFRUTE
and turned away, as
the perfectly ripe Mexican
watermelon melted in the

neutral territory of
my stomach, my curious
hungry human Yaqui
Mestiza stomach, and I

placed the machete
down, wrapped the Mexican
watermelon in plastic, muttering
"DISFRUTE" all the way home.

Los Angeles Airport, June 2007, written in
San Miguel de Allende, México,
crossing the ancient trade route ...

OH PRAISE
(Sacred Marriage)

It started, I think, in late
October, when I journeyed to my
son's wedding in Boulder, Colorado,
Denver Airport, a blizzard blew

in, as I blew in, wearing my
beautiful, wool Peruvian
jacket with animals, sacred
symbols woven every where,

my warm, red, fringed shawl
over my shoulders, my Mexican
silver hand with heart earrings,
my Hopi bear cuff on my right

wrist, beaded rainbow Huichol
bracelet on both wrists, my solar
Mexican calendar ring on my right
hand, I wheeled my luggage through the

star-filled blizzard, air so frozen after
San Miguel de Allende, México, but so
beautiful, I think I was smiling as I walked to
the bus going to Boulder (where my son would

pick me up, my other son waiting for the sacred
marriage to begin), the star falling air, my son's joy,
made me smile, I was pushed hard, off the curb,
almost, almost to my knees, the bruise

on my right upper arm, deep angry
purple, my witness. For one deep
second I wanted to test the killing
blows my deadly 5 foot Chinese from

China kung fu teacher taught me,
just her and I, for a week, "You
and I, we are eagles," she'd laugh,
showing me spear thrust to the

throat, collapsing air way, death —
"Those people have no manners,"
the white man who shoved me smirked,
as I caught my balance, rose, and

decided not to kill him (I'd rather
go to joy than jail for this
sad piece of shit) — the bus
driver shook his head but did

nothing, took my luggage quietly,
as I returned to stand right next to
sad piece of shit, people shifting
one foot to the other, I'd cut in

line to stand next to the
coward, I tried to meet his eyes,
he moved slightly away, his friends
who'd laughed when I'd fallen, were silent —

I stumbled into him, placing a
perfect bee sting in the coward's
ribs, not a death blow but a
re-minder of Earth and Sky, the

power of *those people* to strike
back because those people aren't
cowards, they/we can 't afford to be
cowards, we were trained by our

grandmothers, "No te dejes ... Don't
take any shit," from a piece of
shit. "Fuck," he yelped as the
bus driver took my left arm

very gently, "First in line, miss,"
he smiled, a white man, a good
heart, "had it comin'." Most of
the Boulder white people dirty looks,

young Mexican guy, white students
with backpacks, flash me smiles as
they pass, no one sits next to
me, I'm dangerous, damn straight,

I almost laugh out loud or
LOL as my youngest son taught
me, email speak — but I think
that's when it started, Arizona's

SB 1070 human rights violation,
Those people have no manners ...
a Lakota friend said, "Colorado was
never kind to The People, the

near extinction, genocide, they
did to The People." And I continued
on to the sacred marriage, the
joy of my son, his wife, my family, we

celebrated with deep snow, good
food, champagne, dancing, bad jokes,
heated debates on world issues, me
defending the ancient trade routes that

I keep crossing to return and return,
the sacred Turtle Island, the
sacred presence of deer all week,
a buck with immense antlers to

protect his herd, no fear, looking
back at me, no fear, looking
back at me, I think that's when
it started, sacred deer.

Denver Airport, going home, crossing
the ancient trade routes, a Navajo
painting with the guardian of
the horizon, Changing Woman,

her head a marriage of Sun, Moon,
Stars, and her immense belly, Womb,
holds the zig-zag Cosmos, a deep
dark eye at the center, with

prayer feathers fanning out, her
corn pollen yellow hands and
feet upraised, oh praise oh
praise, on the left a newborn

human, on the right a singing bird
at the tip of tassled corn, and
this is where it all ends, only to
begin again, Changing Woman's

fertile zig-zag Cosmos Womb,
corn pollen yellow hands and feet
upraised, oh praise, The People
continue to be born, to sing at

the tip of ancient, always
new, tassled corn, I think
that's where it started, truly started,
oh praise.

The Pueblo Fifth World,
the Mayan Sixth World,
Kokopelli's ancient song,
oh praise.

*The tiny shadow of Arizona's SB 1070, banning of Ethnic Studies, watching
Professor Soto being jeered and heckled as she spoke at the podium for
graduation, Arizona State University. "Cut your hair, bitch!" a man's voice
slices through. "Cut your tongue," I say, "Changing Woman holds even you in
her sacred zig-zag Cosmos Womb."*

San Miguel de Allende, May 2010

III.

FLOWER

FLOWER
(Dream)

A still vision,
a still dream,
dry cracked earth,
I feel hopeless, sad, the

quiet voice, wisdom,
"The harder the ground,
earth, the more beautiful
the flower." I believe

this wise voice and
dream, you take my
hand, beloved, just my
hand — I see the dark

roots, shoots of light,
I see the urge of
bud, irresistible like love,
to bloom.

San Miguel de Allende, México, 2009

DEAR WORLD,
dear Earth,
dear Angel of Despair and Joy
January 10, 2011

Early morning, as we land in Mexico
City, I see the immense angel, I
blink my eyes, I stare and
stare, it doesn't disappear, it

remains firm, hovering at the
edge of México City's sprawl,
Cloud Angel, Spirit Angel, Angel
Of Despair And Joy, Begging Angel,

Starving Angel, Murdered Angel,
Tortured Angel, Child Prostitute
Angel, Angel Of The Well Fed Loved
Child, Angel Of Loving Parents,

Angel Of Those Who Feed The Hungry,
Angel Of Those Who Give To Beggars,
Angel Of Those Who House The Beaten
Human Body, Angel Of Those Who

Weep For Mercy Compassion
Harvest, Angel Of Those Who
Rage For Poverty's People, Angel Of
The Unashamed Who Bellow, Angel Of

The Shamed Who Whimper, Angel Of
Our Humanity, Angel Present Alive
Every Where, Angel At The Edge Of
México City, I didn't know you

were there until this morning,
December 9th 2010, if I flew
city to city, country to country,
continent to continent, I would

see you firm, hovering, your
immense wings folded softly,
fiercely, your speed of light
eyes balancing the terror,

the wonder, of being
human, you temper our
blindness, give us sight,
Angel Of Diamond Light

Eyes, watching, weeping, gazing,
our strange, stubborn, human
beauty, we persist because of
you, Angel Of Despair

And Joy, at the edge of
México City, every city, town,
village, every Turtle Island,
our Earth.

Los Angeles, The Angels, at noon,
Angel Of Illegal Immigrants, Spanish,
Vietnamese, Chinese, Cambodian spoken
on the streets, many more, do you

sing in every human language,
Turtle Islands, once the massive
Tortoise emerging from primal,
cellular, swirling sea, from

space blue blue blue womb
water, I hear you singing on
the streets of Los Angeles, your
sweet, clear voice pierces my

stubborn, persistent, will-to-live
human heart ... Angel Of Dreaming
Immigrants, Angel Of Native People
Of This Continent (their drums, their

voices, their rattles, dance, song,
keeping us alive, ancient prophecy
coming home, coming home to the
streets of Los Angeles, The Angels, the

Earth, coming home), Angel Of The
Ancient Trade Routes, Angel Of
Shimmering Shifting Borders,
Angel Of The Dispossessed,

Angel Of The Possessive,
Angel Of Diamond Light Eyes,
I hear your sweet, clear voice
piercing even the concrete, flowing

over the Pacific, her still fertile,
swelling waves, piercing every
stubborn human heart, our
Angel Of Despair And Joy,

I hear you singing in every
language, I don't know
the words, what I hear/feel is
your harsh, persistent healing,

O our
Angel Of
Diamond Light
Eyes. Singing.

﹒﹒﹒﹒

Santa Cruz, Holy Cross, ancient
symbol of healing (not the crucified),
night, oh Angel Of Scattered
Families, oh Angel Of Gathered

Families, how do we stand to feel
so much, I wonder, these gathered
memories from sheltered womb to
open door, the delicious, terrifying,

lush, killing, O beauty, O horror,
this human world,
this perfect Earth,
O Angel Of Diamond Light Eyes,

O Angel Of Terror And Wonder,
O Angel Of Despair And Joy,
O Angel Of Scattered Gathered
Families, the families we're

born to, birth to,
the families we create,
O Angel Of Endless Weeping,
O Angel Of Endless Laughter,

we heard your harsh, persistent
voice, healing, and we danced,
oh we danced, to your song,
terror, oh the wonder,

at the edge of Santa Cruz,
at the edge of Los Angeles,
at the edge of México City,
at the edge of every floating,

rooted Turtle Island continent,
at the very edge of our Cosmos,
O Angel Of Diamond Light Eyes,
keep watch as the ancient prophecies,

the ancient trade routes, come
home, keep singing your harsh,
persistent, healing song, every language,
every family, O Angel of Despair And Such Joy.

—— ••••• ——

(Watsonville, Califas, a few
miles south of Santa Cruz) —
my granddaughter works with the
Farm Workers, their children born

two fingers each hand,
im-perfect (as my four
children were born
perfect), spraying of

the fields, their parents
with cancers, dying
to pick the food of
millions, fresh cheap

food at supermarkets, ICE
separating illegal parents from
their legal children, we marched
the streets with Chavez, la Huerta,

over thirty years ago, still they
spray the fields (every where, this
Turtle Island), two fingers to a
hand, the im-perfect children, to

their parents perfect — my youngest
son works with the families of the
dispossessed, the hungry, no
food or refrigerator to hold it, no

place to sleep (bed, mattress), no
place to sit (couch, chairs), no
table to gather (food food), the
country of wealth, abundance,

one in four children are hungry,
Martin Luther King, "The worst violence
is poverty," O Angel Of The Farm
Workers, Angel Of Toxic Food,

Angel Of The Im Perfect,
Angel Of The Perfect,
Angel Of Violence,
Angel Of Healing,

surround each field, unfurl
your wings, tip to tip,
O Angel Of Diamond Light Eyes,
keep watch, our despair and our joy.

To our world, our Earth, every Turtle Island,
every perfect, im perfect human being,
and to our Angel of Despair And Such
Joy ...

San Miguel de Allende, México

DEAR WORLD,
dear Earth,
dear Sixth Mayan World,
dear Fifth Hopi, Pueblo World
March 13, 2011

Those who take no part in the making of world division by ideology are ready to resume life in another world, be they of the Black, White, Red, or Yellow race. They are all one, brothers, sisters. The war will be a spiritual conflict with material matters. Material matters will be destroyed by spiritual beings who will remain to create one world and one nation under one power, that of the Creator. That time is not far off. It will come when the Saquasohuh (Blue Star) Kachina dances in the plaza.
—Frank Waters, *Book of The Hopi*

dear Sixth Mayan World,
dear Fifth Hopi, Pueblo World,
dear, dear sweet Earth,
dear Taknokwunu ... Spirit who controls the weather,
dear Kokyangwuti ... Spider Woman, Creator Woman,
dear Poqanghoya ... Sacred Twin of the North Pole world axis,
dear Palongawhoya ... Sacred Twin of the South Pole world axis,

Two Tsunami dreams in
March, April 1999, my dream
notebook confirms, the heaving
of earth beneath our feet, my

youngest and I, then the
sound of gathered, sheer power,
I've not ever heard before. In
the dream we stand in the One

Place, a place of safety ... Tupkya,
safe place, in my dream. We
watch surfers, people die in
the mountain of water, we weep,

we don't turn away, we witness
the devastation, we hear the
Twins of the North, South Poles,
of Earth's vibratory centers,

call out warning, call out sorrow,
call out Spider Woman's name,
Kokyangwuti. Mother of All Life,
in my dreams I hear them, and

she calls out to Taknokwunu,
Spirit who controls the weather, but
it's too late, it's begun, the shift
of axis, the shift of worlds,

the shift of power, the gathering of
sheer power, the ancient Earth
opens her eyes slowly, the
ground trembles, shudders, dances

awake, trembles, shudders, dances us
awake — so much death, so much
sorrow, the hidden is revealed,
the ancient Sipapuni, the center of

all life, the Place of
Emergence ... what will emerge,
we ask, what will emerge,
what do you weave, Spider Woman?

⸻

We must build a Tipkyavi, womb,
symbolic shrine, altar, for
our Earth, our womb, our Mother, we
must bring objects sacred to

us ... corn of every color, wheat,
slice of bread, bowl of rice, the

egg, glass of clear water, dry
beans, ripe melons, vegetables,

all fruit, the dried umbilical
cords of our beloved children,
all children, every Turtle Island,
every human color, the human

race, every mother's womb as
witness to this birth, this gush
of birth waters, the upheaval
of earth, flesh, earth, the

first startled cry between
her bloody thighs, Tapu'at,
mother, child creation symbol,
bring this too, life, LIFE,

yes, bring this too, life, to Tupkya,
safe place, Sipapuni, Place of
Emergence, the small hole in the floor
of the Kiva, crown of your head.

Poqanghoya, Sacred Twin of the North Pole,
Palongawhoya, Sacred Twin of the South Pole,
hold us in your powerful hands,
our beloved Earth rotates her

new axis, her new dance, her
new birth, her eyes slowly
opening, waking up, she observes
us, the Sipapuni at the crown of

our heads, are they open, are they
closed, are we sleeping, are we
waking, it's time, it's time, it's
time, our Mother wakens, to

push us through her birth canal,
earth upheaval, gushing waters,
the ancient Sipapuni will guide
us if it's open, open our eyes

to terror's wonder. Hold us in
your powerful hands, beloved
Sacred Twins, send out your song, the
Tangakwunu, rainbow.

Santa Fe, New México, Indian Market, 2004,
I stop to admire a young Hopi man's
Kachina carvings, so beautiful,
so perfect, I freeze in the hot

sun, he laughs, bringing my eyes to
his, sheer play, sheer joy, sheer
creation, his mother's son,
I've seen this look in my

own son's eyes, I laugh
with him. "Your Kachinas are
so beautiful, it's like
they're alive." "They are,"

he smiles the smile of the creator.
I buy a small butterfly Kachina,
suddenly he grabs my right hand in
a firm clasp, turning my arm/hand

over, mine on top of his, flash of
smile, creator's eyes, "This is
how we'll know each other in
the next world, sister, the Nakwach."

I'm stunned, his firm grip, without
my permission, his mother's son, my

own sons, I breathe — "I don't
understand, what?" He holds my

gaze — "My people, the Hopi, call
this the Nakwach, remember it,
you'll need it in the next world,"
he laughs. "Show me again," I

smile, he does. "Thank you, I'll
remember, for the next world."
I walk away, slowly, looking
back, waving, my small butterfly

Kachina carefully wrapped, his
firm grip still pressing my hand,
my arm. Talasveniuma, Butterfly
carrying pollen on wings, floats

by, I see bright yellow
pollen wings now now now and
think of what I read this morning (2011),
The traditional Japanese greeting replaced with,

"We are
all in
this together."
Nakwach,

this is how
we'll know
each other in
the next world, Nakwach.

Dear Saquasohuh, Blue Star Kachina,
we will know you
in the next
world, give

me your terrible,
wondrous hand,

we are all in this
together. Nakwach.

To our sister Turtle Island, Japan,
solar energy now, into the Sixth World,
one people, one planet,
into the Sixth World.

San Miguel de Allende, México, 2011

**The quote that opens this poem comes from Frank Waters' *Book of the Hopi* ('Hopi Prophecies'), the words and wisdom which he gathered from "some thirty elders of the Hopi Indian tribe in northern Arizona." He lived with them during the gathering, the gift of their words, ancient knowledge, for this amazing book.

Waters writes in the introduction: "Most of their spokesmen here are old men and women with dark wrinkled faces and gnarled hands. They speak gutturally, deep in their throats and almost without moving their lips, their voices rising out of the depths of an archaic America we have never known, out of immeasurable time, from a fathomless unconscious whose archetypes are as mysterious and incomprehensible to us as the symbols found engraven on the cliff walls of ancient ruins.... This, then, is their book of talk. It is not a professional paper — neither a sociological or psychological study nor an anthropological report. It is the presentation of a life-pattern rooted in the soil of this continent, whose growth is shaped by the same forces that stamp their indigenous seal upon its greatest mountain and smallest insect, and whose flowering is yet to come."

DEFIANCE OF FLOWERS

I sit here, centuries past, eating
breakfast, a tired, hungry looking,
young man, making his errand, carrying
an immense spray of rainbow

flowers, a peacock of
flowers, an altar of
flowers, a defiance of
flowers in his arms, his

stunning child for these stone
lined blocks, the few pesos they
will give him for the gathered beauty,
defiant in his thin, hungry arms, if

Zapata could see him, a
century later, he would weep,
grab his rifle, start a new
revolution, yet they killed

him for his defiance of
flowers, his altar of
flowers, his rainbow of
flowers, and so the poor

still carry burdens and
beauty for the rich,
the masters of this
time, this day, as

I eat my omelette
smothered in salsa,
listening as the well to
do older Mexican man orders

the waiter, the weight of his
class fills his voice,

master to peon, I glance
at him, it's all he has,

no rainbow of flowers,
no altar of flowers,
no defiance of flowers,
no beauty. Of flowers.

His red-blotched angry face holds
these words, though he would deny
it: "I would rather die on my feet, than
live on my knees." Emiliano Zapata

One hundred years after the revolution.

San Miguel de Allende, México
September 2010

LION DREAMS
(Fierceness)

I dream lions all
night, then
I dream rainbows —
I pet the lions though
they're fierce, they
let me, and I enter
the rainbows, all
night between the fierceness
of lions and rainbows.

The fierceness of the world
hides tenderness, the daily
cruelties hide the daily
kindnesses passed around like
bread, simple bread that
fills the stomach, heart,
for years — the fierceness,
the earth's pressure, natural
carbon, reveals the hidden
diamond, the fierceness of
diamonds being born within
diamond womb, between
diamond legs, glittering
diamond hands, fierce
diamond lions. Rainbows.

(From my dream journal, January 2011)

Watching my steps on the
cobbles so I don't

fall, fly — when I first
moved here people rushed to

help me, scraped knee,
embarrassed, then laughing as
they picked me up — today
a man falls in the street,

bus, traffic coming toward
him, human angels quickly
surround him, the lions
lounge in the warm Mexican

Sun. Convulsions, angels bend
to speak to him, touching his
chest, arms, face, he
calms, someone calls an

ambulance, someone offers to
take him in their car, the
lions gather in their sacred
savannah, roar their

fierceness, I long
to pet them in
day light, this
street, as the

human angels
stroke, pet the
fallen man, keeping
him safe from harm.

＊＊＊

To live in a Third World
country, you must live three
years at least, three cycles
around the Great Sun,

you must understand the
language of the country,
the daily music in your
ears, and speak it enough

to joke — you must stop, the
ancient ones begging on the street,
pesos, wait for the blessing, you
must put up barb

wire on your roof, the very
poor live here, and not
take it personally, and when
they scratch your car, the

USA license plate, the same, when
the young man, younger
than your grandson asks, "Do you
want a Mexican boyfriend,"

just laugh, "Hijo, I am
your grandmother" — when one
slow bus passes the other
slow bus, the highway, almost

head-on, you must breathe
deeply, walk over, so carefully,
respectfully, the lounging
lions, stand there, until one

roars, shaking your bones,
stands, moves toward you,
all muscle, deadly, so alive,
now, pet the lion.

As you buy bottled water, the water
from the faucet will make
you deadly sick,
pet the lion.

As you kill the stray
scorpion in the entry,
kitchen, bedroom wall,
pet the lion.

When the taxi driver
helps you unload all
your groceries, tip him,
pet the lion.

When the garbage guys stand
knee deep in it, take yours
from your hands, smiling,
pet the lion.

When the rose man
gifts you an extra
rose, calling you senorita,
pet the lion.

When the ancient grandmothers,
the blind man, bless you
for mere pesos, always
pet the lion.

When people meet your
eyes, human to human,
all day long, yes,
pet the lion.

Is this a Third World country?
Is this the sacred savannah?
Is this a dream of lions?
Is this the fierce diamond world?

Pet the deadly, so
alive, so fiercely
alive, sacred
lion.

San Miguel de Allende, México
2011

DEAR WORLD,
dear Earth,
dear Rainbow,
dear Diamond
March 30, 2011

Always keep a diamond in your mind.
—Tom Waits

I close my eyes and
see it, a rainbow
blinding me, true vision,
light dancing, firing

synapses from the
center of the Earth,
the center where pure
black coal struggles with

gravity, fights with
gravity, dances with
gravity, mates with
gravity, starless womb,

mind, womb, mind, no
light until the tiniest
raw, tiny chunk of
thought, joy, thought, joy

is born,
entices me
to open
my eyes,

to seek
the mirror
of rainbow
of diamond

in the world,
the perfection
in my mind
womb mind,

the tiniest
raw chunk,
what rainbows
it gathers

as I witness
the endless
diamond we
live within —

"Always keep a diamond in your mind."

Seventy-two migrants from
so beautiful Guatemala,
El Salvador, México lindo y querido,
murdered on the USA/México

border, the invisible
border Kokopelli dances
back and forth, back
and forth endlessly —

"Always keep a diamond in your mind."

The gang rapes in the
extravagant, wondrous Congo,
women, girls, boys raped by
men who see no wonder —

"Always keep a diamond in your mind."

The fertile fields of
Pakistan flooded, millions
homeless, parents unable to
protect, feed their children —

"Always keep a diamond in your mind."

USA drones fall on
Afghanistan, Pakistan, birth
place of ancient poets ... who
writes the poems now ...

Rumi, born in Balkh, Afghanistan,
1207 ... "Gamble everything for love,
if you're a true human being," he
sang centuries ago —

"Always keep a diamond in your mind."

Killing wolves in helicopters,
the glittering sacred ice
world, gassing their pups
in dens, what they did

to Native People on
this Turtle Island they
continue with the Wolf
People, their singing clans —

"Always keep a diamond in your mind."

Palestinian gunmen kill
four Israelis in their car,
one a pregnant woman, on
the eve of peace talks,

Hamas calls it a
'heroic operation," the
Palestinians suffer, the
Israelis suffer, together —

"Always keep a diamond in your mind."

Second oil rig explosion,
Gulf of México, those

waters, sacred waters,
dolphins, turtles, every

swimming being that gives
us life, every flying
being that gives us
life, poisoned, our life

giving planet, mother,
poisoned — floods, unseasonal
tornadoes, volcanoes sing
FIRE, Iceland, Indonesia,

our mother, our mother
is waking up with new
eyes, what we've become,
what we've done to

her never-ending beauty,
her never-ending sustenance,
her never-ending dance with
Sun, Sky ... air, gravity ...

"Always keep a diamond in your mind."

Imagine, yes, imagine
ninety-nine lashes on your
back, your tender
body, ninety-nine lashes

because you're a woman,
you're a woman, you're
a woman named
Sakineh Mohammadi Ashtiani,

death by stoning, your
body buried, your
head exposed, blossomed
human fruit, the mind

of a woman, held
captive, lashed ninety-nine
times, imagine, yes, imagine
Sakineh Mohammadi Ashtiani —

"Always keep a diamond in your mind."

In Guinea people not
allowed to grieve their
dead, murdered September 28,
2009, one-hundred and fifty-seven

people, the surviving women raped, their
children, husbands, mothers, fathers,
brothers, sisters, all slaughtered —
Asmaou Diallo speaks of his

murdered thirty-three year old son,
"His name was Mohamed Aliou Conte
and he was a teacher. It's a loss I will
never be able to replace ..."

"Always keep a diamond in your mind."

Xiao Ai Ying, eight month old
living child in her womb, China,
taken from her home, kicked
in the womb, beaten, her

husband, Luo Yan Quan,
witnessed, they killed the living
child in her womb, in her
womb, lethal injection to her

womb, her sacred womb,
her eight month living child, womb,
in China, her empty,
her empty. Murdered. Womb —

"Always keep a diamond in your mind."

The jailing of young men of color, as
a "Well designed social control and legal
discrimination," a young black woman
author, professor states — the rest of their

lives a lower caste, not lower class, she
repeats, lower caste, the new Jim Crow, the
business of prisons, USA higher prison
populations than repressive governments,

as in China, Iran — the corporation of prisons,
the majority of young men of color not
violent, but in prison for possession of
illegal drugs, yet the criminal bankers

go free, the wealthy, the highest
caste, they go free, the ones
who build the prisons, the ones
who take all of our lives, daily —

"Always keep a diamond in your mind."

The migration of birds
changing, falling to
Earth, hundreds,
lost airports

unable
to get a
clear reading,
direction, axis —

"Always keep a diamond in your mind."

March 13, 2011 ... Japan, earth

upheaval, ocean upheaval,
tsunami, so many dead,
nuclear reactors spilling
poison in the air, water, earth

quake earth dance
shifted the axis of our
planet, WARNING
no more nuclear reactors,

my beloved coast of
California is strung with
them, when our Earth
quakes dances quakes

what then, what of the millions of
people, our home, Earth —

"Always keep a diamond in your mind."

They want to cut the budget in the USA,
cut education, teachers, university dreams cut,
cut programs that feed hungry children daily, cut,
cut the rights of women, birth control, 'redefine rape,'

cut, they want to cut the unions that give a working
wage to millions, cut, they refuse to tax the 1% wealthy,
they cut their taxes, CUT, while the rest
become homeless, their children hungry, asked

on a TV show to describe hunger, a young girl said,
weeping with shame, "It's like a hole in my stomach,"
CUT, no food for this girl, all the children
with holes in their stomachs, CUT, yet the

corporations pay no taxes, the ones who build
the prisons, CUT, while they bomb Libya,
March 2011, each missile would fund a school for
a year, CUT, no health care for millions, CUT, send

them to prison, CUT, let them die, CUT —
"Always keep a diamond in your mind."
In Libya, Emon al-Obeidy, woman
in her thirties, crashes a hotel news

conference — "I was raped by fifteen
soldiers for two days, they defecated
and urinated on me, they violated
my honor. My friends are still there,

I escaped this morning." Her face is
cut, her body bruised, she shows the
journalists, as the guards drag her
away, someone covers her head

with a towel yelling, "TRAITOR!"
To the police car, journalists try to
shield her, they shove them violently
away, she shouts, "I am not scared of

anything!" as the door slams shut. This
is the fear-less voice of (wild) wisdom.
"Always keep a diamond
in your mind."

It seems they want to kill the
wild wisdom, born in women's
wombs, the free wombs
of women, that love

who they choose to love,
who fight/bite when necessary,
no apology to survive, thrive,
the Wolf People taught us that,

the Bear People, Hawk and Eagle
People, Snake People, Lion and
Panther People, their songs, their
dances, their dreams, we once knew,

the Pueblo dances at dawn, they
dance for us all, feet touching
Earth, drums, her heart in our
ears, prayer, song, prayer,

wild wisdom remembered,
wild wisdom rising,
wild wisdom resisting
extinction, being born in

women's wombs, the free
wombs of women, starless
womb, fiery womb of my
grandmothers, wild wisdom,

"It's not by accident that the pristine wilderness
of our planet disappears as the understanding of
our own wild natures fades ... The wild feminine (wisdom) is not
only sustainable in all worlds; it sustains all worlds."*

"Always keep a diamond in your mind."

I close my eyes and
see it, a rainbow
blinding me, true vision,
light dancing, firing

synapses from the
center of the Earth,
the center where pure
black coal struggles with

gravity, fights with
gravity, dances with
gravity, mates with
gravity, starless womb

mind, womb, mind, no
light until the tiniest
raw, tiny chunk of
thought, joy, thought, joy

is born, entices me
to open my eyes,
to seek the mirror
of rainbow

of diamond
in the world,
the perfection
in my mind

womb mind,
the tiniest
raw chunk,
what rainbows

it gathers
as I witness
the endless
diamond we

live within ...
Always yes
always yes
always keep

a diamond
in your
womb,
in your

mind,
in your
testicles,
in your
heart ...

San Miguel de Allende, México, 2011

*Dr. Clarissa P. Estes, Women Who Run With The Wolves

TABOO LIFE

Teen with spiky blue
tipped hair, sells me
my first marigolds, sees
my dragon tattoo, says

he wants one, wants to
go to Japan, learn
kung fu, his words,
desires, tumble out, he

is poor, makes maybe
100 pesos a day, maybe
he'll get the dragon
tattoo, his eyes freshly

crushed hope, is this
you, uncle Ruben,
you who left the body at
twenty-one, with so many

young man's desires, your
talents (entire violin concertos
by memory), your taboo
loves in the 1930s Los Angeles

(other young men), your
passions, I imagine to
travel to Paris, Venice, Tokyo,
other wonders — I just

returned from Paris, whispered
your name upon seeing the
Eiffel Tower, and I know
I'll reach Venice, even

Tokyo, so for you, the
teen boy with spiky blue

hair, whispered wonders, a
piece of your spirit

always with me, secret
stories from your mother,
sister, the brilliant boy,
young man, burning with

taboo life, know I
embrace who you were,
who you longed to be,
who you may be. Now.

A mi tio, Ruben Villanueva.
Dia de Los Muertos, 2010
San Miguel de Allende, México

BIRD

You were making fires in
your childhood closet,
small sticks, paper,
cloth, I found the
burn mark, the feathery
ashes on the wooden
floor — I asked you
why, just tell me why,
in my 2nd year psychology,
dreams from my own
childhood, fire as symbol,
fire as scream, fire
as pain, fire as
fiery truth, "I don't
know," you answered, eight
year old voice. You built
beautiful things out of
toothpicks, sticks from
the garden, colored cloth,
paper, in the sink, they
had wings, you called
me before setting fire to
the wings, I stood next to
you as you lit the match,
eyes of fear-joy, as
it blazed for those
minutes we watched together,
the wings turning to feathery
ash. Years later, your twenties,
you told me your father touched
you, touched you, after
the fires, you told me,
you fought back, that
courage in spite of threat
he'd kill us all if
you told, if you told
me, your mother. I had

warning dreams those years,
my early twenties, I protected
you fiercely from strangers,
the stranger was in our
home, in the belly of
that bird you set
on fire. My early
twenties, three young
children, if I had
known I would have
simply killed him, my
friends with sail boat
would have taken the
body far out to sea,
his karma stopped from
harming the next family,
the next children, yes,
I would have simply
killed him (the Buddhist
story of the teacher who
killed a man, on the spot,
seeing he would kill/harm
so many others) — my
dreams warned me of harm,
I fiercely protected you
from strangers, not knowing
he was in the
belly of
your beautiful,
your fiery
bird.

To my beloved son
February 2012, México

SUNLIGHT FIRE

Ashley, when you were
six we rode an elephant
together, we were both
scared and laughing, your
bright self in front of
me, your hair in sunlight
fire. I remember thinking, What
else could be so beautiful
than this child riding an
elephant with me, her large
ears made you laugh, in
Bali they place morning
blossoms behind Ganesh's
elephant ears, light incense,
offerings of food to Ganesh —
May there be no obstacles.
Today we held signs of
protest, OCCUPY SANTA
CRUZ, we shared one, making
us laugh, I DON'T NEED
SEX MY GOVERNMENT FUCKS
ME EVERY DAY, car honks, we
wave, dance our sign for
the one in five children hungry
daily, parents cannot
feed them, lost their union
jobs, the 1% buying the
largest yachts in history,
the 99% standing here,
riding the enormous elephant,
Ganesh, May there be no obstacles,
we ride this elephant together,
twenty-four years later,
granddaughter, healer, Amazon,
dancer, your hair in sunlight
fire — we yell, "WE ARE THE
99%" fiercely, laughing,

Ganesh leading the
way, we all ride,
May there be no
obstacles, May there
be no obstacles,
May there be no
obstacles,
for the 99%
world wide, as
we ride into the
Sixth World.

To my granddaughter, Ashley
Santa Cruz, Califas, October 2011
Into the Mayan Sixth World, 12/21/12

LEANING INTO THE WIND

Old union organizer, president
of the Ironworkers, your son
(my first husband, teenager) was
terrified of you — the night

we came to dinner, my three children,
your son, after the gourmet
meal cooked by your noncomplaining
wife (who tied your

boy with clothesline, gagged for
hours, too much trouble/energy), you
sat by yourself, your favorite
chair, your wife bringing your

whiskey on the rocks, you
sat alone, your son watching
something on TB quietly, in awe
of your presence, my kids teasing

each other, undisciplined monsters
(your blood-shot eyes say) — I can't
help myself, I come and sit
next to you, the other chair

(reserved for men, clearly),
silence, shock, especially your
twenty-six year old son, also
an Ironworker, who walks

those high wind beams, leaning
into the wind not to fall, sensing
when the wind will change direction,
but your son is not the president,

you are, so I ask the obvious —
"How did you become president of
the Ironworkers?" You glare at
me, I hold your gaze, waiting —

"Mary, bring another whiskey, the
bottle!" She brings it, confused —
"Give it to her, she wants to talk,"
you laugh loudly, no kindness.

"Do you drink whiskey?"
"I think your son would like one," I
see he's edged close on the couch,
silently, a beaten dog/boy/dog.

"He can get his own." The bottle
between us — he refills his glass,
I sip mine. "Before unions men
just lined up for work, the bosses

picking only the youngest, the strongest,
and if you worked your youth out
for them, what did they care?"
you boom, drowning out the TV,

my three kids stop to listen,
especially the older two. "I saw
men of thirty with families, no job,
kids starving, so when I came

to this West Coast, I got into
construction, bad pay, bad
hiring, the bosses still in
charge, the no good bastards."

You eyes dare me to correct
your language, my kid's eyes
wide — I stand to refill my glass —
"Bring more ice, Mary!" you command,

and pick up the bottle, motioning me
to sit — the ice in a bowl, you refill
my glass. "So me, a French Canadian
who loved the high beams, my

Cree grandma said us Indians
know the wind ... (edge of gentleness,
memory)...I got good being an
Ironworker here on the West Coast,

got to know the Longshore Harry
Bridges" — your son stands to
fill his glass, you let him, not
looking at him once — "I saw

men beaten bloody, some
dead, the bosses hired
thugs when we tried to
unionize, and when the scabs

came through our lines we
beat them bloody, some
dead, they had families, too
bad, time for unions, real

pay for real work no matter how
old you are, ya get me?"
I nod yes, sipping my whiskey.
"The no good bastards wouldn't

be picking and choosing who would
work, who wouldn't work, so
Harry Bridges, the Longshoremen,
all the unions, took over

San Francisco, the West Coast,
damn right, shipped those
scabs home in meat lockers,
and now a man earns a decent

living." "And women, teachers,
nurses, Teamsters," I add.
He holds my impudent gaze — "Yeah,
women too, that's right, we all

got families, we all
got to work for a livin',
so we got the bastards out,
got the unions in, and it

wasn't easy, someone your
age (you slice an angry glance
at your son) wouldn't
know." You pour me more

whiskey, I sip, your son
doesn't dare ask for more, he
will take off for a week or
two and drink, if I'm lucky

I'll beat him to the pay
check, I'm twenty-four with
three children, going to community
college — "Ya got to know the wind,

ya get me?" Years later you would
weave a blanket of beautiful design,
after you retired, your wife gave
it to me, a gift from you.

I gave it to my son, your youngest
grandchild, a gentle man, a man
of heart — I've not ever crossed
a picket line, my older children

joined me with the Farmworkers on
the streets of San Francisco years
later, still they struggle, still
the racism, and today Wisconsin

stripped its unions of bargaining
rights, Arizona/Alabama with
their racist laws — but I
remember you, a man who wove

the first bloody union
blanket, ferociously fought
for with human lives, that
families wouldn't starve as

the no good bastards chose
the youngest, the strongest,
to work that day, fuck
the rest — yes, I get you,

Remie Goulet, I really
get you, the way the wind
blows, lean into it, carry a
warm blanket.

In memory of the General Strike,
Bloody Thursday, July 5, 1935,
The Mission, San Francisco.
Remie Goulet worked on the Golden
Gate Bridge, where he also said
Ironworkers fell to their deaths
building it, that wind. And to the
OCCUPY movement, now, QUE VIVA

San Miguel de Allende, México, 2011

HEART OF A JAGUAR

Rolling my carry on into a
bar, Los Angeles International,
a take off margarita, it
gets stuck, I'm tired, hot,

irritated, long lines, getting
frisked aka felt up by a
woman young enough to be my
granddaughter, "Kinky," I sigh, a

Samurai looking guy leaps to
his feet, picks my carry on up
with one finger, smiling, places it
next to him, obviously seeing my

face, "What are you having?"
I decline, he won't let me —
"A very cold margarita." He
laughs, "Coming up," and orders it

for me. Victor, the Mexican bartender,
and one for him, people staring in
some kind of awe, at him, not
me ... Is this guy a rock star or

something, I wonder, I have no
idea, let it go, we sip our drinks,
perfect and cold, he fields
some calls, speaking in Spanish,

French, a language I don't
recognize, he turns off his IPhone,
tells me it's Hebrew, he's from
Israel, his gaze is direct ... the

way a jaguar is direct ... should
he eat you or has he had his
fill today, the human smile,
we talk, people continue to

stare, that awe, and I fully
realize his energy has entirely
enveloped the room, me included,
I don't mind as long as he's not

hungry, we talk, two more
cold, perfect margaritas. His
voice is soft, smooth, precise —
"I'm an Israeli Commando, I'm

going home but first Sweden,
France. I'm engaged, my final
fling," he shows me her photo,
striking, beautiful, strong. "She'll

be the mother of my children, I
hope to see them grown ..."
He tells me some hair raising stories,
his missions, and I wonder if

he'll have to kill me, I've told
him I'm a poet/writer, he must
know I'm taking mental notes, it's
beyond my control, but he also

must have known he could trust
me, I wont' reveal them here, he
won't allow me to pay for my
drinks or the tip, "Taken care

of," he smiles, no jaguar — he
tells me his father was Mexican, his
mother Jewish, stories of his
family, the Holocaust, his

father's courage to come alone to
Gringolandia, they met dancing
salsa, his smooth dark skin,
deep green eyes (ah the

jaguar, the beauty), his
body, his muscles, dwarf me,
he sponges oil delicately from
his pizza, offering me a slice, a

man breaks in, "Haven't I
seen you in films, sorry to
intrude," his girlfriend swoons
next to him. "You have me confused

with the wrestler-actor, I think, it
happens," Jaguar reveals his
perfect teeth, human smile,
they want to join us (him) —

"Sorry, I'm catching up with an
old friend, take care." Voice
back to softness, smooth
purr, back to stories, his

childhood, mine, he laughs, "You
kicked some butt, mujer, I like
that in a woman, like my Mom,
strong." He orders a bottle of

fizzing water for take off,
slices of lime, Victor clearly
knows him, admires him, discreetly, the
fearless Jaguar holds my

gaze, I forget to breathe —
"You know, I don't want to
die, I want to live to be a
very, very old man with

grandkids all around me, but
I won't allow (his voice slightly
breaks) Israel to be pushed into
the sea, no, never." He stands to

leave, me in 30 minutes, he smiles,
kissing me so softly on my left
cheek, "Wait," I paw through
my immense travel purse, find it,

"Here, take this, she'll keep
you safe ..." "Quan Yin, of
course, I'll put her on my altar
at home, gracias Alma Luz,"

"De nada, _____," he places
Quan Yin in an inner pocket, smiles,
entirely human, turns once, waves,
his Samurai presence makes people

stop, stare, wish to eat him,
clearing a path for him to glide
through ... he's big, muscled,
entirely graceful. Jaguar.

· · ·

His essence will be born into my
novel, not his stories, a dinner
of an Israeli Commando, a
Mexican Muslim art dealer,

a Nicaraguan journalist orphaned by
war, a Japanese grandchild of
Hiroshima traveling the world, hiding
healing crystals, praying, "Never

again, never again," a Mexican
Mafia drug lord, killed his
father at fourteen, beating his
mother bloody, his childhood, a

thirty-four year old Toltec
physician in love with an older mixed
blood teacher/photographer, traveling
in México, this all night dinner

in México, the Mexican Muslim's
mansion, the surprise for his
guests after dinner, vino, hookah, behind
a Japanese screen, the

sorrows of the world revealed,
Star of David on an old worn
child's jacket, photos of concentration
camps, mushroom cloud death over

Hiroshima, death squads in Latin
America and more ... Someone says,
"I wonder what the name of the child
was, who wore that coat?"

"Solomon," the Israeli Commando whispers,
"my grandfather's name." Everyone echos
"Solomon," a song to remember "Solomon" —
"My first son will be Solomon, Solomon."

The teacher/photographer wishes she
could take a photo of him, his
lovely fiancee who weeps,
"Solomon, yes he'll be named

Solomon." A further screen
reveals the beauty of the
world, photos, paintings, a life
size shimmering Buddha, so

calmly, in the center, the
teacher/photographer's sweet,
handsome son meets the young Japanese
woman's eyes, she will live,

they will love each other,
one daughter, one son, dawn
finds them laughing, I
think the Jaguar would

like that, Quan Yin in
his inner pocket, he keeps
her there, not his altar, close
to his heart.

San Miguel de Allende, México, May 2011

IV.

FRAGILE SILK

FRAGILE SILK
(Dream)

Something calls me to
the roof, something
terrible, something
wonderful, so I

climb slowly,
slowly, cautiously
to the roof,
each stair I

memorize. I
hear silence, I
hear singing, I
hear weeping, I

hear laughing.
Photos of my
life nailed to
the wall, nothing

fancy, just
the truth, just
the truth of
living, of

loving, of
hating, of
fighting, of
surrendering,

always oh
always to
the wonder of
love, all

her terrible, all
her wonderful
guises. A circle
of golden

butterflies hold
the air, hold
my heart, each
breath, fragile

wings, fragile
silk, suspended,
I'm held by
love.

San Miguel de Allende, México, 2012

PARIS

(This Body)

What does Paris mean
to me, what waits,
why do I dream
those ancient
streets, ancient
as San Miguel's,
México, cobble stones,
stained glass churches,
sacred sites of the
Goddess, sister island,
Turtle Island singing
me always Home, this
sacred Earth, this
sacred planet, I want
to set my feet on
and walk.
Before I leave this
body, I want to
walk dance walk dance
the sister islands,
the Turtle Island body
that once held us
completely in her
arms.

(Mexican Hat Dance)

For my mother who
danced the Mexican
Hat Dance at her
sister's wedding, a
Baptist church, no
dancing the rule, their
father a Baptist minister,
their mother a Yaqui
curendera, the church
basement, I remember my
mother, Lydia, grabbing some
one's hat, tossing it on
the floor, laughing, her
red red lips, lifting her
skirt over her knees and
dancing the Mexican
Hat Dance to every
one's shock, they made
her stop dancing the
Mexican Hat Dance,
tears in her eyes,
she walked out the
door laughing, her
red red lips refusing
to cry.

There's an old photo, I'm
twelve, she thirty-eight,
it surprises me to see
I'm shorter than her, my
mother, I come to her
shoulder, so I must
be four foot 4 inches or
so, I thought I was
bigger than my mother,
taller than my mother,

I was always saving her
life as in *Super Girl*, she's
wearing the 2nd hand
fur coat she bought at
the Salvation Army, I'm
wearing a weird plaid 2nd
hand dress with a 2nd
hand black sweater, sea
shells sewn onto it, I
like it, the ocean I
ride to on my stolen
bike — I'm pointing to her
2nd hand fur coat, laughing,
she seems to be laughing
with me, so happy in
her fur coat, her fifties
hair style, her red red
lips waiting to be
loved.

⋯⋯

She left her 93 year old
body this week, she
couldn't remember her
past, people's names,
people's faces, she
left her 2nd hand body
for pure light, pure
love, finally I see
her naked lips
smeared with joy,
she pauses to remember
her life, Super Girl's
laughing face, every face
she tried to love,
including her own, and all
there is, pure light,
the sound of a ranchera
tempting her to dance at

her sister's wedding, and she
dances one more time,
pure light.

────

(Moon Light)

Her hands on the piano
keys, early morning,
Moonlight Sonata, trained
classical pianist, church
pianist, her father's church —
I was six, enthralled
with the beauty of
concentration on my
mother's face, I would
wake up to the beauty
of her fingers, the rare
peace reflected like the
moon, Moonlight Sonata,
early morning, before she
used her fingers for numbing
typing, those pre-feminist
days, the promising seventeen
year old composer, just
a woman, just a Mexican
woman, her rented piano,
early morning.

────

(In Your Honor)

You never returned to
your parent's birth
place, México, where I
now live — you never
left this Turtle Island
continent, you never

flew on a plane or
drove a car, you
always laughed at
my adventures, the stories
I told you to make you
laugh, my only power
(to be loved), my final
Super Girl power — I'm
sixty-six, a grandmother,
and I will dance in Paris,
in your honor,
they'd better
hide their hats,
this one's for you,
Lydia Villanueva.

To my mother, her beautiful red lips,
and the dance she gifted me —
October 2010, México

IN PARIS

Look long at what pleases you.
Look longer at what displeases you.
—Colette

Outdoor cafe facing fountain,
light rain, students
without umbrellas, laughing,
children dancing between

rain drops, gathering gold
leaves to wave like
flags, beautiful women
wearing boots, dark ponies,

one in skin tight black
leather leggings, tiny skirt,
over the knee black leather
ponies, black leather jacket,

long purple feather earrings,
shiny black mane, galloping, a
man saunters toward the
fountain, laughing to himself,

turns, arms raised to
each rain drop, all black,
bright red shoes, he
leaps and turns, stealing

my smile, my gaze,
echo of Artaud, Anais Nin,
Colette, Proust, the
red shoes they wore,

the magic of the city on
his feet, he dances,
twirls, leaps, laughs,
arms raised for a moment, I

want to follow him,
photograph him, the bright
red shoes, his laughter,
but I let him go, the

magic of this city,
timeless sensuality, joy,
Colette's full mocking gaze,
her wonder, I see.

Beautiful African man,
car next to me, me in a
tour bus, he in a slick
suit, smiling up at me, such

charm, such confidence,
I look away, what I usually
do, then glance back,
he's still smiling, I

meet his gaze, smiling,
he blows me a kiss,
drives away, hey the
brothers in Paris are

fiiiiine, no memories
of being strung up,
sold on the block,
castrated, the slavery

DNA, wow, I smile to
myself, that's what a
free African feels like,
yet the black men of my

country slowly transforming
the sorrow, the poison,
as are my brown brothers,
into the joy, the confidence,

to blow a kiss
to the human
of their choosing, oh
beauty oh beauty

oh beauty,
I blow you all
a kiss from
Paris.

Brown/black sisters, their
stilettos, knee high boots,
drum their stunning dance,
the street hums with

celebration, I hear Shange's
words in their passing, "I
found god in myself and I
loved her. I loved her

fiercely." Slavery, rape,
genocide, hatred, healed,
oh healed in that strutting,
confident walk, I murmur,

"Work it, sister, yeah
work it," smiling as they
strut by — low cut
black dress, black

nylons, stiletto heels,
gold hoop earrings,
gaze of a queen, a
Goddess, I'm staring,

look around, quick glance
a few men. This morning, my
birthday, men waving at
me, smiling as I pass, why

aren't they gawking at this
20 something surreal beauty, I
wonder — I ask the man next
to me, our conversation (pretty

stunning himself, black
leather to his boots, small
diamond right ear) — "Why
aren't men falling off their

chairs with this kind of
beauty passing by ..." I
pause, gather truth ... "and
why are men flirting with me,

old enough to be her mother" —
(really grandmother, my
granddaughter 29, as is my
youngest son, I keep this

to myself), ah vanity, I
laugh — "In the USA she'd
have to hire armed guards."
He smiles, taking me in, "Here,

we love the ripened woman
and the ripened man, a
rarity, that integration of
wisdom and innocence. That

refusal to become bitter, I
hope to achieve that, and
this is why you write,
no?" "Yes," I laugh,

tears stinging my eyes,
yes, and he pours
me white wine from
his bottle, 11a.m.

"To the ripened woman,
to the ripened man,"
he smiles, and we drink
to that.

"I found god in myself
and I loved her.
I loved her fiercely."
Work it.

Wearing my Santa Fe black
Panama hat, Paris morning,
men smile, blow me kisses,
the word chapeau I recognize,

they love my hat, where
else in the world do men
love your chapeau — elegant
older woman on Metro,

Dior glasses, Dior purse,
outfit, elegant cane,
meets my eyes, smiles with
approval, briefly.

The Pantheon, Voltaire's
bones are here, the
ones that held him up
to walk, write, love,

just his bones,
just the glowing dust of
his bones, the one
who wrote, "Paradise is

where I am," is gone,
the bones don't speak,
his spirit, his words
speak, and Colette, she's

not in the Pantheon with
all the honorable men,
she's buried (her bones) in the
earth she loved, become earth,

air, the sky we breathe,
flying things soar on
her breath, and Jim
Morrison sings harmony,

"Paradise is where we
are, paradise is where
we are, oh paradise
is always

is always
is always
where we are are are
par a dise we are."

Luxembourg Gardens,
a magical nymph pond,
sculpted fairies and
demons, grandmother trees

loosing leaves to be
come young in spring,
surrounded by arches of
trained ivy, sedate

ducks in pond, a small
boy tosses a love letter
to the indifferent ducks,
he screams with delight

as they peck it once,
not food, swim on, you
grab a metal
chair, sit where you

wish to view the magic,
shadows, last Sun sings
to the fairies and demons,
"Soon they'll be gone, you'll

be free to bathe, make love,
create beauty, chaos,
until they come with their
metal chairs

to witness
the magic
you weave
toward dawn."

· - ·◄◆►· - ·

I come closer to the
fountain, the large
faun-demon hovers
over the pool menacingly,

lovingly, below him
two lovers entwined,
making love for-ever, a
young couple sits next to

this beauty/warning, she
sits in his lap, laughing, he
holds her, intimately, laughing,
they pay no attention to

the faun-demon, why
should they, this is the
moment to love, this perfect
moment. This garden.

I stumble on. My last
day. Paris. This enchanted.
Pool. The faun-demon
(blesses me). He does.

And I realize, for
once, I look longer
at what pleases,
the simple beauty

of love, I look
longer at what
pleases me, my last
day. In Paris.

October 2010, Paris

NEXT INITIATION

*The important thing is to be able
at any moment to sacrifice what
we are for what we could become.*
—Charles Du Boc, French critic

Every seven years, our
cells become entirely
new, our body, familiar
flesh, a stranger waiting

to become the next
phase of becoming, at
seven I gave dancing
shows for visitors, my grand

mother, others were
offended, my strange dance,
she knew I had to dance my
memory, let it go, when

I visited Bali, I
recognized my dance fifty-seven
years later — my words at twelve
lost to me, stark grief, dead

planet, Mamacita pure
light at the end of the couch,
my bed, her funeral day, all night
she comforted, taught me, one

more time. Pregnant at fourteen,
daughter, son, son, I modeled
in San Francisco, terrified of los
gringos, almost nineteen, but

more terrified of hand I stabbed
coming through my window, a woman
raped nightly, violent projects
we left, my earned model money, found

my words, volcano
poetry, at twenty-eight,
first husband monster shed,
poetry on my farm, growing

all things, Mother Corn lettuce
tomatoes potatoes grapes plums
apples squash broccoli chickens
(layers, fryers) dancing steer (beef)

the pigs (ham), all the growing children,
all the growing poetry,
all the lost words found,
tears/laughter/shooting stars,

the final son at thirty-six,
sacred snow, sacred fire,
treasured child, ancient child,
wolf dog, sacred lakes, first

novel at forty-two,
second husband friend and
lover, jealous man, after
twenty years I chose my

Self, alone all one, I
journeyed the world all
one, often lonely, often
whole, often abandoned,

often cherished — I journeyed
to Mamacita's México lindo
y querido, the essence of
la vida, my Toyota sedan,

giving every thing away, Give
Away Eagle Feather blessing
me, driving down from Santa
Fe to San Miguel de Allende,

living Whirlwind Warriors
guiding, guarding me, sacred
healer's face to the Sun,
silent desert, ancient home,

wandering Yaquis, this Yaqui
in a 55 mile per hour metal
dream, taking Mamacita's spirit
home, the white dove at sunset,

the roof, church bells on
the hour, she stayed glowing
white in darkness, four
sunsets, gone — from the

girl dancer at seven, womb
mother of four treasured ones,
woman who found her words,
books of poetry, novels, stories,

teaching beloved students, as
I approach my
seventieth year, the
dancing girl of seven,

I approach my new body,
I wonder what
I'll become,
she laughs,

high in the trees, calling
me to climb as high as I
can, that vision, the next
initiation, the next

phase, what I must
sacrifice to meet the
beloved stranger,
my true Self,

who waits for me
to climb, Eagle
Feather, blessing
me, she laughs.

San Miguel de Allende, México
January 2012

FURY MEMORY BIRTH
(Beauty)

Guanajuato, México ... Costa Rica

Saying goodbye to mi
casita, shuttle drive
through cobble streets,
La Virgen murals, altars,

every where, the beauty
of good bye — can
I ever live without La
Virgen's presence, beauty

on the highway, Sunday
markets, the small towns,
families gathered outside
church, cradling babies, a

fresh maize stand, kids
waiting, slathered in butter
(real butter), mayonnaise, chili
sprinkled, some lime, Madre

Maiz devoured with joy,
aguas fresca — strawberry,
pineapple, watermelon for
thirst — I say good bye

with my eyes, my heart,
my taste buds, memories
of my children when they
were home, barbeques on

the beach, enormous
appetites, healthy children,
their friends — I remember
full moon walk on the

beach, north coast, Sonoma
County, our farm, the
quiet, the stillness, gentle
high tide full of light, the

light leaps, into darkness,
glittering with furious
life, a salmon remembering
her way home, full of

fury, memory, birth. This
is how we live, I think,
waiting for my plane in México,
if we are fully awake,

darkness into light. (I glance
down from the shuttle, small
ribbon of light, pure white
crane sipping sun light, a man

sitting, dark earth,
awake, witnessing
the fury of
beauty).

Manuel Antonio, Costa Rica.

White face monkeys outside
my room, I offer water
melon, one bares her
sharp little teeth, following

me, she wants my
plate, all of it, I
laugh, "No way, little
monkey dude," she

feels like my mother's hungry
ghost, not properly mourned,
hard to love, though I
mourned her, remember the

best in her, but can't
give her my plate, no one
gets the plate, no one, we
can share, take less than

half, but no one gets the
whole plate — I remember you,
mother, little greedy monkey,
such lonely needs, and

offer you watermelon, banana
and laugh at your
daring, your best, where
I inherited my playful monkey dance.

Sacred crescent beach,
womb waters, salty
warm, surfers, swimmers
being born by the

minute, deadly rip tide
holding Shakti's balance,
watchful dark brown skin life
guard, his whistle, waving

us back, Don't die today,
don't fight the tide,
don't fight the womb
waters, come back, come

back, don't die today,
be born, be born, this
second,
beauty.

What makes us want to
live, I ask the little
monkey ... Shakti, watchful
life guard ... is it

fury, memory, birth,
or is it Shakti
ever present ... live live
live now, oh beauty.

The Healer

She comes soft, strong,
always the sign of
the healer, her massage
table close to the tide,

she feels like my daughter
at this age, her twenties,
this soft strength power,
the healer — she has her

small daughters with
her, each one beautiful,
future healers, soft light
power in their eyes, not

encouraged in my country,
small daughters dressing like
small, sad, sexy women,
the center of their eyes, light

gone hard, false power,
soft healing power not
honored, not encouraged,
not recognized by their

mothers with eyes light
gone hard, gone bitter,
gone lost, what chance
for the daughters to know

their own soft light
power, the healing.
I lay under her hands,
she feels my life, I feel

hers, she finds my sorrow,
my pain, my joy, fierce
memory of my body, years,
and yes beauty gathered,

her healer meets
my healer, her
memory, my
memory, soft

light power,
furious beauty,
this moment,
now,

why I
was born,
face to salt
sea womb,

oh Shakti,
oh fierce
memory, soft
light power

born in
me, born in
you, the healer,
my beauty.

The Waterfall, Sacred Rainforest

Riding Sargento to the
waterfall, I think they
gave me el caballo,
the horse with a mind of

his own — the others
drink from the creek,
I wait, he doesn't, the
horses shouldn't eat, the

others don't, Sargento stops
to pull leaves from branches, I
try to stop him, he laughs,
I pat his stubborn brown

hide, tell him (in Spanish,
Costa Rica), he's a good
caballito, gracias for the
ride through heat, sacred rainforest,

he begins to allow me
to ride him, guide him, stop,
go, he reminds me every
being has their dignity,

their yes, their no, as
Che the tour leader bellows
information, knowledge like a
professor in his classroom,

stories to and from the
waterfall, the pool so
cold from a hidden source,
cold in this heat, this

cold beautiful yes/no, I
swim because Sargento
brought me here, guided by
Che's stories, his

knowledge of sacred
healing plants. I tell
him he's a teacher, "No, I'm
always learning," he smiles.

"That's why you're a teacher,
we teach, we're taught, otherwise
we become dead," I smile with
him. "OR STUPID!" Che booms,

laughing loudly, his
eyes softly furious, his
eyes holding memory, birth —
Sargento quivers, tosses his

head with laughter, wild
caballito, I have not tamed
him, or him me. We simply
gather yes/no beauty.

La Mar Viene ... The Goddess Comes

"La mar viene ... the Goddess comes,"
the teen picks up my lounger,
slides up the sand, my
favorite restaurant, I order

tacitos, cerveza, the troubadour
sings for us, for me, songs of
love, we all join in, "Besame, besame
mucho," as the Goddess

finds my
feet, warm
salt, one
more swim,

back to eat,
to sing, songs
of love, 2-for-1 margaritas,
la mar viene, beauty, the

young woman has
wings on her back, I have
wings on my back, she
looks sad and alone, I'm

happy and alone, final
day, Shakti's warm salty
womb, home, I give her
my second margarita, she

laughs, lights up, gifting me
a daughter's smile, we toast
my final day, la mar, we toast
her first day, la mar, and

we laugh, this moment
of surprise, this lovely
young woman with wings,
we toast. This beauty.

La Madre Volcano, Alive

Her hair swirls with heat
and ash, visible to all
eyes — "Usually misty this
time of day, we're lucky,"

I'm told — I feel her
mountain fiery womb
creating earth, creating
planet, creating furious

memory, birth, beauty,
she holds my heart, my
womb, as I walk down
fiery flowered trail to her

hot springs, her gift,
womb to womb. Silence.
No one else. Blue Morpho
Butterfly flutters. No one

else. La Madre
Volcano, alive.
Silence. Birth waters.
Blue Morpho wings.

Womb to womb.
Memory. Fury.
Heat and ash.
Our beauty.

San Jose, Pura Vida

Barbed wire every where, every
house, every business, late
night drive to hotel, a teen
face down on cement, I

want to stop, driver
smiles, "He'll wake up,
señora." I return two weeks
later, rainforest, la mar, to

barbed wire, packed streets,
foot in hole, I fall,
people stop to pick me
up, pointing out holes all

the way down the street,
I laugh, "Okay," walk into
the main, immense plaza, policia
on scaffolds, watching, angels

on roof tops, watching,
bird sculptures, pages on
wings, books, pages turning
in the afternoon winds,

peace bird with golden
children reaching for wings,
small children with butterflies,
stars, sun and moon, painted

by clown, parents laughing,
bride and groom, so young,
smiling at the camera, ragged
poet shouting his poetry, sees

me listening, gains courage,
"You need me to shout these
words, you need me to shout
these words to you, and so I do

until you listen, listen ..." (Spanish)
I fall in love, right there,
this barbed wire city, drug
induced teens, balanced by

PURA VIDA, the poet who
shouts his words, his frightened
audience, yet they listen,
lost ancestors, in his loud

desperate courageous
insistent ragged poetry
barbed wire.
Beauty.

México City Airport, March 20, 2012, 12:30 pm.

I love the power of the
Mother, as she begins to
dance, arms raised, her feet
stamping swaying swimming,

the waiter pouring my wine
stops, I say, "Feels like
an earthquake," he leaves
me the bottle, I pour a full

glass of cabernet to go with
my Greek salad, people
running out the door, children
in hand, I don't feel the

deep stamp of her foot
so I stay sipping, eating, a
woman walks in with
black plastic garbage bag,

continues to sit, her and I, we
seem to be holding the moment,
La Madre's dance, we smile,
people return, people weep,

we smile, this woman
and I, holding the
moment, terrifying
wonder. Beauty.

San Miguel de Allende, México

An ancient woman climbs
the hill to the central
plaza, bunches of pure
white lilies strapped to

her back, I chase her,
I chase mi Mamacita now
dead, spirit transformed,
fifty-five years ago, but I

chase her, her pure white
lilies strapped to her
back. She turns her face to
meet mine, an eye patch over

her left eye, her right
eye meets mine directly,
she takes the pure white lilies
into her hands, showing me,

telling me (in Spanish), "I picked
these this morning, how many,
hija?" I think I chased her
for this word, this simple word,

hija … I pick two bunches,
paying her 100 pesos, she never
smiles, her right eye meeting
mine. Only once have I seen

this direct wild gaze, this
burning eye; in the mountains
I picked up a dazed Merlin
Hawk, crashed into my cabin

window, woke up, talons
perched on my open palms, I
held her weight close to my
womb, slowly slowly to tree

trunk, I saw my palms
ripped open to bone, slowly
slowly, she hopped, perched,
rested, spread her three foot

wings, flew. Terror.
Wonder. Burning eye.
I am the daughter of
lilies. Beauty.

San Miguel de Allende, México
March 2012
Into the Sixth World ...

QUERIDO POPOCATEPTL

The villagers call you
father, brother, uncle, son —
I call you lover, my
ancient lover — flying in
to México City I saw
your snowy peak, you
didn't fool me, I felt
the heat of your body,
your lava, your core,
your longing for my
touch, ancient lover,
the Earth danced beneath
my feet, our Mother, la
Madre, she knew nothing
could keep me from you,
your body, your lava,
your core, the ancient
memory of our union.
I dream your body, gift from Earth,
Sun, Moon, every Star, I see
your molten eyes, your molten mouth,
your molten hands, your molten sex, lava
bright, meteor bright, first eruption,
genesis of our longing. I am coming,
wait for me, I am dreaming,
wait for me, I am singing,
wait for me, I am dying
to receive. Your burning
body. Lava.

San Miguel de Allende, México, April 2012

* Two weeks after la Madre's dance, Popocateptl began to sing to his
lover, Iztaccihuatl, fire and ash.

QUETZALCOATL'S RADIANCE

I live in México
because fireworks wake
me up pre-dawn,
Quetzalcoatl shimmering through

sky window, these
fireworks loud like
gunfire, someone's
died, left the body,

someone beloved, they
explode, they weep
for two hours, through
the day, and no

one calls the police, every
one understands some
one's left their body, some
one beloved is gone. I

dream through explosions,
wake to loud, joyous
mariachis in the distance,
a marriage, family gathering —

I live in México
because death and
life hold hands,
dancing, singing, exploding

with grief and joy —
I live in México
because every car stops
for the funeral procession,

a singer/guitarist sings
the beloved's favorite
songs on the way to
the cemetery, where

families will gather, Dia
de Los Muertos, to
welcome their tender spirits
home, from babies to

elders, a feast on the
graves they decorate,
joy/sorrow equally,
beauty, song, candles,

tiny stars flickering all
night long as spirits
come to taste tamales,
tacitos, tequila, cerveza,

fresh limes, oranges,
sweet cakes, where
the father of his spirit
teen, grave decorated with

little cars, dancing
muertos, bottles of
empty Victorias (his
favorite), some full,

proudly shows me his
handsome boy, I can't
weep, his smile of
pure joy —

I drove to México
in spring 2005, the
fear color codes of
my country, endless

wars on some enemy,
my dreams filled with
mourning women, holding
spirit children, sons, daughters,

only sorrow, only grief,
no graves of marigolds,
feasts, sorrow/joy,
death holding hands

with life, dancing, singing,
weeping, exploding
pre-dawn journey of
the beloved, all day

into the night, mariachis
leading a wedding party to
more joy, holding hands
with life, death, life —

I live in México
to remember,
to witness
simple human

joy sorrow joy,
those without my
country's great entitlement,
the leaders, the shameless

1% who would haul
off the mourner with
explosive weeping, singing,
who allow one in five

children in my country to
be hungry, who prefer
the poor to die (very)
quickly, while mouthing

how much they love their
country, care for its people,
send the neediest young to
kill/die for their oil wars,

want to control the
sacred wombs of women,
the constant enemy,
the constant fear,

unhinging our young, our
unbonded to our Mother
Earth young, bringing
automatic weapons to

schools, universities,
playgrounds, now
theaters where the masses
go to dream, the manufactured

dream of Holly Wood
dream, all humans need to
dream, many have forgotten how to
dream, vision —

I live in México
because a Huichol family
in full brilliant rainbow
dress motioned me in front

of them, the market, I
thanked them but no, their
rainbow smiles insisted,
and the woman helped

me unload my full
cart, their few carefully
selected items waited, she
smiled her rainbows, I

smiled mine, "Gracias,
gracias, gracias,"
I kept saying, why
I live in México.

I live in México to feel
full sun on my face,
full moon light, shadow,
Quetzalcoatl's radiance.

San Miguel de Allende, México
July 2012

MADRE COATLIQUE EN JUÁREZ

Listen. My skull
rattle skirt as I
pass by. The rattle
in my hand, life, death,
life, death, rain,
listen. Where I walk,
where I dance, the
dead spring to life,
each girl, young
woman, a tender
flower, a spiky
flesh tearing cactus.
Listen. As I pass,
how their spirits
sing, "Madre Coatlique,
I am born again, I am not here,
do not mourn me here, I am flesh
made new, Madre Coatlique."*
Listen.
My skull rattle skirt,
the rattle in my hand
brings life, death, rain,
and to the men who took
precious life, a curse
on their line for seven
generations. Listen. A
blessing to those with courage
to heal it. Listen.
Thunder,
lightning,
skull rattle,
rain.

Listen. I want my
daughters, granddaughters,
to know how to (ancient
martial arts) break the
trachea, push bone
into brain, their life
giving, death giving
hands. I want them
to know they hold
life/death in their hands,
to fight for the Self
is sacred. To fight
for their children is
always sacred. To wield
a sword, a knife (carry it),
sacred. Listen.

You were born from the
sweet darkness of
my womb, the journey
of my pain, vagina.
I do not ask for
respect, I claim
it. I am your warrior
ancestor, Madre Coatlique.
Thunder,
lighting,
skull rattle.
Rain.
Listen.

To the hundreds of raped, tortured, murdered girls,
young women, of Juarez, México, that they may begin
the dance of Madre Coatlique, the ancient Goddess.

San Miguel, de Allende, México 2012

*From the marvelous, wise book — *Women Who Run With The Wolves*.

DEAR WORLD
Dear Earth,
Querida Madre Coatlique
September 21, 2012
(Equinox)

Dear World,
dear Earth,
dear Cosmos,
dear Ixchel,
dear Quetzalcoatl,
Querida Madre Coatlique,

I've walked outside to
witness police beating
teens in my country (USA),
pointing their guns at

me, twice, "This is none of
your business, go inside,
lady!" "Stupid bitch!"
putting their guns away

as I continued to stand
at the curb, witnessing,
then following them to
police station, filing

my complaint — one in
Santa Cruz (Califas), blonde
teen, returned to thank me,
his grandfather a local

judge — the other in Pacifica
(Califas), brown teen, was
set free. In San Francisco
I witnessed in my

backyard with many
neighbors, a man
with knife to wife's
throat, small children

screaming beside her,
her eyes of silent terror,
I grabbed my sharpest
knife, in my pocket,

told my teen daughter,
"Call the cops, give
them our address, lead
them there," she did (she

became an ICU nurse,
of course). Driving in San
Francisco, my three children
under twelve, I witnessed

a beautiful black man
in dashiki begin to run,
grabbing woman holding baby,
her purse strap wrapped

around her wrist, dragging
her down the street,
men watching like TV,
I aimed for him,

"Mom, you're going to
hit that man!" I hit
him, split second, chose
not to kill him, he

limped away (my sons
work healing families),
the woman holding the
baby, the four year old

screaming behind her, became
my best amiga, cancer
taking her one year later,
her two boys became

mine, moved to the country,
my farm. My grandmother,
Jesus Villanueva, full blood
Yaqui de Sonora, trained

me to be a dreamer and
a warrior, she saw my
life — I stabbed my
uncle, her brother, from

México, at five, trying to
molest me, she protected
my Spirit, "I told you to
leave her alone." I knocked

my insane/drunk step
father out at ten, strangling
my pregnant mother, she
and my brother lived, all

my life I've fought
for my self,
for the other,
Jesus Villanueva's gift

to me, "The Yaquis are
undefeated," she used to
tell me (in Spanish), her
eagle eyes on fire,

the fire she passed on
to me, white light all
night she came to me the
night of her funeral, I

refused to weep, wore a
red blouse, threw a
red rose on her coffin, no
grave stone, years later

I returned to find her
bones, #13 her marker, now
I know the sacredness of
the number thirteen, Mayan

number of blessing, Native
number of strength, the
balance of self and
other, the number of

fire, her gift to me,
fire, to witness, to
act, to dream self
and other, other

and self. Now
I know
I am
the 13th

ancestor, where
I leap, where
we leap, into the
Sacred Sixth Sun

on fire
we leap
we swim
this nightly

wave of
fire, of
flood, of
drought, of

war, we dream
of peace, we are
the 13th ancestor, self
and other, other and

self, sacred 13th
ancestor, we
are, witnessing
fire.

San Miguel de Allende, México

CEREMONY

Climbing the Sixth Sun,
Sacred Sun Pyramid,
straight up, warm
Sun, cool morning

Wind God pushes me
up, I pause to
breathe deeply,
drink water, a boy

of four behind me
begins to cry, he's
thirsty, forgot to
bring him water, I

offer mine, he smiles
and drinks — work at
the top, not able
to climb to the top,

a great-grandmother in her
eighties is helped to
the almost top, her
family bracing her,

no one is bracing me, it
seems to be my path,
to climb the Sacred
Pyramid of the Sixth

Sun alone, the only
(grown) child I miss
is my youngest, but
la vida calls him,

as it should, his own
family, families in great
need, a daily warrior
in the world, and I

needed to come alone,
all one, to greet
the Sacred Sixth
Sun, and one thirsty

four year old boy.
Unable to climb to the
top, I circled, my
rattle singing, next

year I will be a
great-grandmother and
no one will brace me,
yes they will love me,

that's allowed, maybe
in my eighties when I'm
a great-great-grandmother,
maybe, right now the

waiter has read my mind,
plays native flute, drums,
rattles, my birth
day gift, so well

deserved, bird song,
rattles, all day
sacred white butterflies
followed me, yellow

monarchs, little bees,
brash young men, "Hola
hermosa ... I have a special
gift for you ... Mi amor ...

Take it it's free," I
didn't do my usual come
back, "I'm old enough
to be your grandmother,"

now "I'm old enough
to be your great-grandmother,"
I just laughed, right now
the music is only rattles,

the sound of sweet
bones, the ancestors
winging home, I'm a
baby, I'm an

ancient, I'm not
born, I'm dead/transformed,
I'm newly born, always
to the song of rattles,

sweet bones, winging us
home, dancing us home —
I just told the waiter, my
grandson, youngest son's

age, "This music, flute, drums,
now only rattles, is
perfect, gracias."
"It suits this place,

your presence." (He
doesn't bullshit me
with senorita, I've
been called senorita all

day, I laughed, they
wanted some thing, my
smile, my money, my
life) — he's an eagle

dancer, a deer
dancer, a wind
dancer, a sun
dancer, I know

his mother loves him,
he loves his mother,
the women in his
family, sacred, he

knows I need the
sweet bones of the
ancestors, a pure
chocolate cake woven

with fruit, drizzled
with honey/chocolate,
a perfect birth day
cake — I sit by the

pool, too cold to
swim, a clay flower
painted señorita, I
laugh.

An older man, probably
my age, asked me if
I'd done ceremony on
the Pyramid of the Sun,

without thinking I answered
yes, the two silver bracelets
symbols of Quetzalcoatl,
Sacred Sixth Sun,

I bought, 50 pesos each,
the third a gift,
he smiled, "Fuego,"
fire should always

be a gift, the
entire day, a
ceremony, the gift of
water and fire,

I hear the laughter of
my four grown
children, grandchildren,
great-grandchild in the

cosmic womb dreaming,
the ancestors singing
the rattle song, all
my friends, some over

thirty/forty years, my
students seeing me whole, I
see them whole, we are the
gift. We are the ceremony.

⋯⋯⋯

White butterflies,
ancestor souls,
guide me/us to
Quetzalcoatl's Temple,

some know it,
some don't,
yet we all
arrive, Quetzalcoatl's

Spirit laughing in the
young grass, the
large rocks tiny
red ants carry to

their mound/pyramid, bleeding
cactus fruit/flowers, ancient
clouds/air Quetzalcoatl
breathed, laughing, I

hear him laughing,
some times weeping
for his children,
I sit facing

steps that he
climbed (still
climbs, Full Moon
Mother blessing him),

flanked each side Sacred
Snake, Sacred Jaguar,
Sacred Eagle, Sacred
Shell, I hear him

laughing, take out my
bird rattle, Quetzalcoatl's
flute I bought here
thirty-four years ago

at the foot of Pyramid
of the Sun, lone vendor,
almost sunset, newly
married, we climbed to the

top that day, each
playing it, we became
Gods, today I play
bird rattle, snake/eagle

flute, weaving tears and
laughter, loss and gift,
folly and wisdom, marriage
to the Other, marriage

to the Self, silence
and song, stillness
and such dancing, today
I became fully human.

We all
we all circle
we all circle the
we all circle the sacred

Pyramid of the Sun
rattles in hands
flutes to our lips
laughing weeping silent

singing limping dancing
we all
we all enter
we all enter the

we all enter the Sixth
we all enter the Sixth Sacred
we all enter the Sixth Sacred Sun
we all enter the Sacred

Sixth Sun
bracing each
other up
together

together
together

Teotihuacan, México
Into the Sixth Sun
October 2012

ESSENCE

I am filled with you,
Skin, blood, bone, brain and soul.
There's no room for lack of trust, or trust.
Nothing in this existence but that existence.
—Rumi

Hot springs, La Gruta (small sacred
grotto where water gushes, where the
tangible light plays, lives), early morning
I swim, float, swim in ecstasy — in la gruta

I stand under the pounding waterfall as
it's hard heat massages my wings, my folded
wings that dream the world, the cosmos, my
life, la vida ... I stand in the tangible light as

she blesses me, I chant to the molecules of
gushing water, streaming tangible light, my folded
iridescent wings, my unfolding ripening blossoming
heart body heart body, I chant to all

that exists, existence. This. A tiny iridescent
hummingbird pauses to sip the tiniest yellow
blossoms, the sexual penis — shaped purplish
fruit dangling from the fertile banana tree,

a crown of tiny bananas begin to sprout,
and underneath the sexual penis-shaped purplish
fruit, the tiniest so sweet yellow blossoms,
the iridescent hummingbird sipping this ripeness,

filling its swift body with this, existence,
this potent fertile blossomed ripening essence,
existence. This. Ripening. This.
Filling (fertile potent) essence.

I want to touch your feet, to kiss
them, to remember your
first steps, your footprints
glowing in the world.

I want to caress your calves, your knees, your
thighs, to lick the salt gathered there, the
years I didn't know you were alive, yet
I dreamt you, heard your voice.

I want to explore your chest, the map of
your longing, your vast desire to be free — and
your back, flaring up to your secret wings that
dreamt you to the moment we spoke.

I want to follow your fearless neck and
pause for centuries to gaze into your open
face, your ancient (always new) eyes that
mirror my own ancient (always new) eyes like

the sun
the moon
the stars
the soul.

I want to touch your mouth with my mouth,
I want to touch your tongue with my tongue,
I want to remember the lava that flows
in me in you in me in you potent fertile —

I want to sip that fertile potent essence —
I want to know your ripened purplish fruit, your
delicate yellow blossoms ... my iridescent wings
unfold, dreaming you closer, more clearly, I sip.

I want to make love, yes, to your secret wings that
dreamt you to the moment we spoke. I want to
fill myself with you — I want you to
fill yourself with me.

That potent
that fertile
that existence.
That. Essence.

Always to The Beloved,
In time ...

San Miguel de Allende, México

THIRTEENTH WOMB
Unity
(Dreams)

I dream rain at dawn,
I wake to rain at dawn,
I wake to fireworks,
I wake to drumming, rattles, singing,
I wake to Feathered Jaguar,
the pre-dawn sky,
the powerful paw, rustling
feathers, waking me ... .

Someone's fallen off a
cliff, the great Madre
Mar pulls back,
revealing her life,
her death, her 13th
womb exposed, I
grab her hand, pull
her up, she swims
ahead of me, a tidal
wave of mud, churned
earth rises before
me, I know what to
do, I dive into
death. Life.

San Miguel de Allende, México, 2012

ABOUT THE AUTHOR

Alma Luz Villanueva was raised in San Francisco's Mission District, mainly by her curandera/healer Yaqui grandmother, Jesus Villanueva. Jesus taught her to recite poetry by heart (in Spanish) for church. Though she writes in English, Villanueva says that "the language/meaning is rooted in Spanish, and the Yaqui prayers I heard my grandmother sing every morning to the new Child Sun. Without Mamacita Jesus, no memory, no poetry, no stories."

Villanueva began to publish poetry in the late 1970s, winning first place in poetry with the University of California at Irvine's Chicano Literary Prize. Her books of poetry include *Bloodroot, Mother, May I?, Life Span, Planet* (Latin American Writers poetry prize), *Desire, Vida,* and *Gracias.* "Crazy Courage" was included in *Best American Poetry,* 1996.

Villanueva's novel, *The Ultraviolet Sky,* received the American Book Award, and was listed in *500 Great Books by Women.* Her second novel, *Naked Ladies,* won the PEN Oakland fiction award, and was excerpted in *Caliente: The Best Erotic Latin American Writing.* Her third novel, *Luna's California Poppies,* was recently excerpted in the anthology, *Califlora.* Stories from Villanueva's collection, *Weeping Woman: La Llorona and Other Stories,* have been included in several anthologies, most recently in *Coming of Age in the 21st Century.* Her most recent novel is *Song of the Golden Scorpion* (Wings Press, 2013).

Her fiction and poetry have been included in numerous textbooks, from elementary school to university, and has been the subject of Masters/Ph.D. thesis papers in the USA and abroad.

Villanueva taught fiction/poetry at the University of California, Santa Cruz, as well as Cabrillo College in Aptos. She has been a guest writer at the Naropa Institute, the University of California at San Diego, Stanford University, Pacific University, and many other institutions. She now teaches in the MFA in Creative Writing program with Antioch University in Los Angeles.

When she is not traveling to do readings, workshops, seminars, etc., Villanueva lives and writes most of the year in San Miguel de Allende (Mexico).

To find out more:
www.almaluzvillanueva.com

Wings Press was founded in 1975 by Joanie Whitebird and Joseph F. Lomax, both deceased, as "an informal association of artists and cultural mythologists dedicated to the preservation of the literature of the nation of Texas." Publisher, editor and designer since 1995, Bryce Milligan is honored to carry on and expand that mission to include the finest in American writing—meaning all of the Americas, without commercial considerations clouding the decision to publish or not to publish.

Wings Press intends to produce multi-cultural books, chapbooks, ebooks, recordings and broadsides that enlighten the human spirit and enliven the mind. Everyone ever associated with Wings has been or is a writer, and we know well that writing is a transformational art form capable of changing the world, primarily by allowing us to glimpse something of each other's souls. We believe that good writing is innovative, insightful, and interesting. But most of all it is honest. As Bob Dylan put it, "To live outside the law, you must be honest."

Likewise, Wings Press is committed to treating the planet itself as a partner. Thus the press uses as much recycled material as possible, from the paper on which the books are printed to the boxes in which they are shipped.

As Robert Dana wrote in *Against the Grain,* "Small press publishing is personal publishing. In essence, it's a matter of personal vision, personal taste and courage, and personal friendships." Welcome to our world.

WingsPress

This first edition of *Gracias,* by Alma Luz Villanueva, has been printed on 55 pound Edwards Brothers "natural" paper containing a percentage of recycled fiber. Titles have been set in AquilineTwo and Cochin type, the text in Adobe Caslon type. This book was designed by Bryce Milligan.

On-line catalogue and ordering:
www.wingspress.com
Wings Press titles are distributed to the trade by the
Independent Publishers Group • www.ipgbook.com
and in Europe by Gazelle • www.gazellebookservices.co.uk

Also available as an ebook.